GATHERINGS

Bronwen Wild

HODDER AND STOUGHTON

LONDON SYDNEY AUCKLAND TORONTO

Acknowledgments

The author and publishers are grateful to the following for allowing text to be used in this book:

Daphne Rae/Hodder & Stoughton (p 5); Laurie Lee/Chatto & Windus (p 10); Valerie Avery/Wm Kimber & Co (p 12); Collins (p 17 – Prayer); Erma Bombeck/Chicago Sun-Times (p 18, p 55); Richard Bode/Reader's Digest (p 20); Tony Winter (p 23); Rumer Godden/Macmillan (p 25); Lilli Palmer/Verlag Schoeller & Co (p 27); Laurie Lee/André Deutsch (p 35); Keith Waterhouse (p 37); James Clarke (p 43, p 50, p 77 – Prayers); David Higham Associates (p 44, p 46); Jonathan Cape (p 49); Molly Cheston/Watson, Little Ltd (p 57); Pete Hamill/New York Post (p 60); Bill Naughton/Thomas Nelson & Sons (p 62); Vanessa Wager (p 64); Karen Wallis (p 65); Harvey Kirk/Weekend Magazine (p 74); Virginia Black (p 80); Monica Dickens/Michael Joseph Ltd (p 83); Hans Peter Richter/Penguin Books (p 71, p 86); Sharmila Modha (p 90)

Cover photo (Crete) by Gareth Stanfield.

The publishers have made every effort to trace copyright-holders but if they have inadvertently failed to acknowledge any copyright, they will be pleased to make the necessary arrangements at the first opportunity.

For Graham, my family and all my friends at Rooks Heath.

British Library Cataloguing in Publication Data

Gatherings.
  1. Schools – Exercises and recreations
  2. Schools – Prayers
  I. Wild, Bronwen
  377'.1   LB3015

  ISBN 0 340 39763 2

First published 1987
Second impression 1987

Typeset by Graphicraft Typesetters Limited, Hong Kong
Printed in Great Britain
for Hodder and Stoughton Educational
a division of Hodder and Stoughton Ltd, Mill Road
Dunton Green, Sevenoaks, Kent by
Page Bros Ltd, Norwich

Contents

Preface	4
Introduction	4
Only More Love	5
Martin Luther King	8
Kids Everywhere	10
Old Age	12
Getting Away	14
In The Beginning	16
Mothers	18
Varied Talents	20
Easter	22
On A Winter's Morning	23
He's Not Tough, He's Gentle	25
To the Top of the Mountain	27
A Piece of Bread	30
They Too Have Their Place	33
Winter Time	35
Christmas	37
You Are Like That	40
Loving, and Being Loved	42
Holidays	44
'Ah Just Wanted To Put Things Right'	46
Communication (or Lack of It)	49
A Beginning (and an Ending)	51
Children's Charter	53
A Mother's Love	55
Foolish Dares	57
'You're Going Home, Not Knowing?'	60
Finders Keepers	62
When Dad Left Home	64
Maybe Tomorrow	65
See Me	67
The Most Gentle Person	69
Fool's Paradise	71
You're a Walking Marvel	74
Just Gossip?	76
A Smile	78
Blessing the Bride	80
The Art of Marriage	82
'Ere, Where's Me 'Andbag?'	83
Auf Wiedersehen	86
I Remember	90
Author Index	92
Index of Titles of Readings	92
Music Index	93
Subjects of Readings	94
Suggested Themes	94

Preface

Recently we have heard much yet again about the 'hidden' curriculum and it is probably true that many judge our schools by the unspoken code of morality. I hope our children do follow the example of good and caring staff, but some things have to be spelt out clearly.

Mrs Bron Wild came to us on school practice from college, and is now Deputy Head. Over these years I have had the privilege of both participating and delighting in many of her assemblies. I am very glad she is sharing them with others.

Betty I. Burkitt
Headmistress of
Rooks Heath High School
South Harrow 1962–86

Introduction

Gatherings is a selection of readings drawn from a variety of sources to be used for assemblies or classroom work. The readings present a wide view of life which will appeal to the adolescent audience.

The music is merely a suggestion to set the scene of the reading. It may be omitted or alternatives substituted.*

The prayers are short and to the point, in keeping with the readings, and suitable for multi-faith assemblies.

My thanks to those young people who have not only shared in these *Gatherings*, but who have also contributed to them.

B.W.
1987

---

* The *Hooked on Classics* tapes (KTEL: Louis Clark conducting the Royal Philharmonic Orchestra) form a useful collection which covers all aspects and moods.

Only More Love

Music

'Oxygene' by Jean M. Jarre (Polydor 3100 398)

Reading

extract from Love until it Hurts *by Daphne Rae*

A woman lay dying on a Calcutta pavement. Her feet were half eaten away by rats and ants. She had been lying there for days and no one had taken any notice of her.

Then a nun came along. She was a tiny woman, dressed in a white sari which hung loosely about her and covered her head. She walked quickly, for she was always in a hurry. Her name was Mother Teresa.

When she saw the woman on the pavement she stopped. Full of pity, she picked her up and carried her to a nearby hospital for treatment. They told her there that the woman was too ill and poor to bother about. Besides, they had no room. Mother Teresa pleaded with them, but they said there was nothing they could do for her. However, she would not leave her patient, and set off for another hospital. But it was in vain. The woman died.

In a world that is increasingly in conflict, modern day pressures make us withdraw into ourselves. The purpose of life is made even more mysterious through war, hatred and greed, and the poor become victims of injustice. There are many who philosophise, who try to forget when we see posters of starving, disease-ridden children of the Third World. We try to forget that there are millions who are dying of starvation, TB, leprosy and all the diseases that result from malnutrition. When we realise the truth, we are afraid, because the problem is too big.

Mother Teresa was not afraid, even though she knew the enormity. She just went ahead in faith and did what was immediately in front of her. Throughout the world, the nuns and brothers of the Missionaries of Charity, too, have no fear – through their faith in God they grow in strength and love.

What is it that makes the world award the Nobel Prize to Mother Teresa and her Missionaries? She is the epitome of the Order she has founded, and she is respected and revered by people of all faiths. She has spirit and determination, she faces the problems of life and acts on what she sees. 'Wherever there is a need among the poor and destitute in India, Australia, the Middle East or anywhere in the world, I will set up a home and send my nuns and brothers.' They work with the destitute and dying, the mentally handicapped, the alcoholics, the drug addicts, aborted and abandoned babies. God is supplying young men and women to the Order. They come as they know that God demands 'their all' and they give their all willingly with love and joy.

Mother Teresa never writes articles, but she makes speeches. This is part of a speech she gave in the packed Cathedral at Delhi:

'Do you know of the houses that are run by the Missionaries of Charity? There are now over a hundred and forty in India alone.

In Calcutta, there is a Hindu temple to Kali at Kalighat; we were given the guest house belonging to this temple for the care of those who were dying in poverty.

Thirty-nine thousand patients have been brought to Kalighat, and of these nineteen thousand have died, yet they never complain, they never die in despair, for they are given love. It is we who say 'thank you' to them for allowing us the privilege of serving them.

I brought in a lady from the streets – there were maggots crawling out of her wounds. These wounds were washed and she lay dying. What would I have done if I had been that woman? I would have tried to attract attention, but all she said was 'thank you'. I learnt love and humility from her.

There was a Hindu woman who had eight children and no money to buy food. I took rice and curry to the family. The mother divided the food into halves, and took a half share to a Muslim woman who also had starving children. 'Their need is as great as ours,' said the Hindu woman. I was not surprised that she had shared her food, but I was surprised that the Hindu woman _knew_.

Do we know our neighbour's needs in this pluralistic society? Or are we kept at home by television?

Our order of Missionaries of Charity have a home in New York. One day they were called to go to a flat where a number of milk bottles stood outside the door. Inside the flat they found a dead woman. No one knew her name – they only knew the milk which she ordered.

Love begins at home – in the family – with your neighbours. 'Love one another as I have loved you,' said our Lord.

Are we helping the poor, the lonely, the oppressed?

People want to see Christ in others. Therefore, we must love Christ with undivided love until it hurts. It must be total surrender, a total conviction that nothing separates us from the love of Christ. We belong to Christ.

The Missionaries of Charity choose to live in poverty in order to help those who are poor. Thus the fourth vow which each Missionary takes is to dedicate his or her life in giving themselves wholeheartedly and totally to the poorest of the poor.

In Calcutta our sisters and brothers feed seven thousand people daily. One day there was no money to buy rice. No one knew how the food would be provided, but they had faith, and without warning several truck loads of bread arrived from a cancelled schools' function. The hungry and destitute had never eaten so much bread.

Recently, during a period of sugar rationing, a child arrived clutching a small bag of sugar. 'I do not need this, please take it to give to the poor,' he said. He had saved his own ration for four days.

There is so much love in us all, but we are often too shy to express our love and we keep it bottled up inside us. We must learn to love, to love until it hurts and we will then know how to accept love.

We must be a channel of peace.

We must love until it hurts.

We must be Christ.

We must not be afraid to show our love.

India is recognising the works of love, so too is the world. The Nobel Prize was awarded for love – is this not wonderful? If you love, then there is peace in your soul and joy in your heart.

Love God, love God in the womb. Love God in the unborn Child. Love God in the family. Love God in your neighbour. Love until it hurts.'

Prayer

Let us bow our heads and in a few moments
of quiet, let us consider what we have just
heard...
Let us preach you without preaching, not by words
But by our example...

Martin Luther King

Music

'Battle Hymn of the Republic' sung by Joan Baez
(from Joan Baez in concert Part 2: *Vanguard VK79113)*

Reading

'I Have a Dream'

That piece of music has become closely identified with the life and work of Martin Luther King.

Martin Luther King, the grandson of a slave, was a Baptist pastor who received a Nobel Peace Prize and was murdered at the age of thirty-nine years. The reasons for his award and for his early death were the same. Martin Luther King was a moderate, humble man who preached and practised non-violence and he gave his people something they had never known – hope for the future.

On 20th August 1963, 250,000 men and women from all over America gathered at the Lincoln Memorial in Washington DC. They had come to attend the largest demonstration ever held in America in support of civil rights for American blacks. When the main speaker of the day was announced, that vast crowd fell completely silent.

A short, rather stocky black man quietly took the stand. In a prepared speech, he described the problems of blacks in America throughout history. He then continued: 'Now is the time to rise from the dark and desolate valley of segregation to the sunlit path of racial justice. Now is the time to make justice the reality for all of God's children.

But there is something that I must say to my people who stand on the warm threshold which leads into the palace of justice. In the process of gaining our rightful place we must not be guilty of wrongful deeds. Let us not seek to satisfy our thirst for freedom by drinking from the cup of bitterness and hatred. We must forever conduct our struggle on the high plane of dignity and discipline. We must not allow our creative protest to degenerate into physical violence. The marvellous new militancy which has engulfed the Negro community must not lead us to a distrust of all white people, for many of our white brothers, as evidence by their presence here today, have come to realise that their destiny is tied up with our destiny and they have come to realise that their freedom is inextricably bound to our freedom. We cannot walk alone.

I say to you today, my friends, even though we face the difficulties of today and tomorrow, I still have a dream. It is a dream deeply rooted in the American dream.

I have a dream that one day this nation will rise up and live out the true meaning of its creed: "We hold these truths to be self evident; that all men are created equal."

I have a dream that one day on the red hills of Georgia the sons of former slaves and the sons of former slaveowners will be able to sit down together at the table of brotherhood.

I have a dream that my four little children will one day live in a nation where they will not be judged by the colour of their skin but by the content of their character.

I have a dream today.

This is our hope. This is the faith with which I return to the South. With this faith we will be able to hew out of the mountain of despair a stone of hope. With this faith we will be able to transform the jangling discords of our nation into a beautiful symphony of brotherhood. With this faith we will be able to work together, to pray together, to struggle together, to go to jail together, to stand up for freedom together, knowing that we will be free one day.

This will be the day when all of God's children will be able to sing with new meaning "Let Freedom Ring". When we allow freedom to ring, when we let it ring from every village and every hamlet, from every state and every city, we will be able to speed up that day when all of God's children, black men and white men, Jews and Gentiles, Protestants and Catholics, will be able to join hands and sing in the words of the old Negro spiritual, 'Free at last! Free at last! Thank God Almighty, we are free at last!'

Prayer

'Martin Luther King was possibly this generation's most inspiring martyr, dedicated to brotherhood at any cost and dying in the certainty of the ultimate victory of Love over Hate!' (*From a sermon by Paul Ostreicher*)

'Help us to come to understand that non-violence is a powerful and just weapon, which cuts without wounding and ennobles the man who wields it. It is a sword that heals.' – *Martin Luther King*

Kids Everywhere

Music

'Friends Medley' by The New Seekers
(from Together: *Polydor 3170 161)*

Reading

from Cider with Rosie *by Laurie Lee*

The morning came, without any warning, when my sisters surrounded me, wrapped me in scarves, tied my boot-laces, thrust a cap
on my head, and stuffed a baked potato in my pocket.

'What's this?' I said.

'You're starting school today.'

'I ain't. I'm stopping 'ome.'

'Now, come on, Loll. You're a big boy now.'

'I ain't.'

'You are.'

'Boo hoo.'

They picked me up bodily, kicking and bawling, and carried me
up to the road.

'Boys who don't go to school get put into boxes, and turn into
rabbits, and get chopped up on Sundays.'

I felt this was overdoing it rather, but I said no more after that. I
arrived at school just three feet tall and fatly wrapped in my scarves.
The playground roared like a rodeo, and the potato burned through
my thigh. Old boots, ragged stockings, torn trousers and skirts,
went skidding and skating around me. The rabble closed in; I was
encircled; grit flew in my face like shrapnel. Tall girls with frizzed
hair, and huge boys with sharp elbows, began to prod me with
hideous interest. They plucked at my scarves, spun me round like a
top, punched my nose and stole my potato.

I was rescued at last by a gracious lady – the sixteen-year-old
junior-teacher – who boxed a few ears and dried my face and led me
off to The Infants. I spent that first day picking holes in paper, then
went home in a smouldering temper.

'What's the matter, Loll? Didn't he like it at school, then?'

'They never gave me the present!'

'Present? What present?'

'They said they'd give me a present.'

'Well, now, I'm sure they didn't.'

'They did! They said: "You're Laurie Lee, ain't you? Well, just you sit there for the present." I sat there all day but I never got it. I ain't going back there again!'

But after a week I felt like a veteran and grew as ruthless as anyone else. Somebody had stolen my baked potato, so I swiped somebody else's apple.

Prayer

We pray for kids
Everywhere in the whole world.
Some have no houses
Some have no food
Some are so sad.
We have problems too,
So we hope that you can
Do a few things to help
Kids everywhere.
(Based on a prayer from *Treat Me Cool, Lord* by Carl Burke)

Old Age

Music

'When I'm Sixty Four' by The Beatles (from Sergeant Pepper's Lonely Hearts Club Band: EMI Columbia TC PCS 7027)

Reading

'Gran' by Valerie Avery

Nevertheless, I liked Gran; she was so different from Mum. Because Mum left early for work in the mornings I would go downstairs and talk to Gran while waiting to go to school. She sat in her armchair before the fire, wearing an old red dressing gown, cooking her breakfast; she toasted bread on a fork, or held a rasher of bacon before the flames with one hand catching the drips of fat on a slice of bread which she held in her other hand. When it was cooked she put it on a plate which had already been used twice that morning: first for Steve's breakfast of bacon and mushrooms and then, when he left for work, Grandad cleaned the plate with a slice of bread while waiting for his bacon and eggs to be dished up. The over-worked plate was smeared with yolk and bits of bacon curled round the edge. While Gran ate I did all the talking. I told her about school.

'We're learning French now, Gran. *Quelle heure est-il?* D'you know what that means?'

'Gawd knows.'

'It means: What's the time?'

'Oh does it. Can't see the point meself. Steve says they all talk English in every country, and 'e's seen almost every country on 'is bike, so what's the point? But tell me more about that science teacher of yours.'

I envied Gran sitting in her chair with the cat at her feet, toasting her breakfast in her warm, sleepy kitchen. I wished I could be her and not have to go to school, while she kept wishing she were my age. Her motto was 'Here today, gone tomorrow.' Mum said it was bad for me to listen to her morbid talk, but I was fascinated by tales of hospitals, funerals, and death.

'This woman 'ad no inside. She 'ad to live on boiled eggs and water, and 'er 'usband 'e 'ad no arms, blown off in the war they was, so 'e 'ad to manage with two 'ooks. Turned you up to look at 'im, but the funny thing is they both lived to a ripe old age, whereas 'is brother was a big 'ealthy bloke, strong as 'orse 'e was, never 'ad a day's illness in 'is life. One day 'e 'ad 'is dinner, big eater 'e was, 'e 'ad steak and kidney pud, that was 'is favourite grub, an' 'e says to his wife: "I think I'll take the dog for a walk in the park." So 'e goes out. But 'e never came back. Dropped down dead outside the bakers 'e did. Just like that.'

While she talked to me, she washed her face and hands in a large mixing bowl which she stood on the kitchen table and was filled to the brim with boiling water. The red, strong-smelling soap rested on a saucer while she covered her face with a creamy pink lather, then sluiced it off, cupping her hands several times with water and sounding, as she put her face into it, as though she were drinking a bowl of soup. With water dripping from her chins and her eyes stinging with soap, she groped around blindly for the towel, tugging first at the tablecloth, then at the curtains, until she realised that it was still hanging on the line over the range.

'Give us the towel, there's a good girl,' she'd say. 'Quick now. It doesn't matter if you can't find it, anything 'ill do, so long as it's not yer Grandad's combinations.'

It took her about half an hour to dress herself because she wore so many layers of clothes; petticoat upon petticoat, all different colours and different lengths, waited in a queue to move up nearer to her skin each morning, and each was fastened by dozens of hooks and buttons.

'Yer need plenty of clothes when yer gets to my age, because yer feel the cold something terrible yer do. Goes straight to yer bones it does and gives her rheumaticks if yer don't wrap proper.'

Finally she combed her grey, greasy hair that was usually lank, but if she was going to a special jumble sale that day, or to her old age pensioners' club, she forced it to curl by using her iron curling tongs. She would sit in her arm-chair and wait for the tortuous tongs to turn red-hot in the fire then, catching a strand of hair in a scorching grasp, she twisted the tongs round and round until they could go no further. For a few seconds they were held taut while she waited for the miracle to happen.

'Does it hurt, Gran?'

'Not 'alf," she said. 'Burnin' me brains out, it is, but it's worth it. The 'otter the tongs the longer me curls stay in.'

'Won't your hair catch alight?'

'It will if I keep 'em in too long. There, I think I'm done now,' and she pulled out the tongs leaving behind a long grey, sizzling sausage.

Prayer

Help us to think about good things to do like helping each other, or helping old people. Really, we don't like not doing anything, but we need you to point us in the right direction.

Getting Away

Music

'Day is Done' by Peter, Paul and Mary (from The Best of Peter, Paul and Mary: Warner Bros CWF 651)

Reading

'Getting Away' by Hilda Warren

I was in trouble again; this time for being saucy to my grandmother. I hadn't thought I was being cheeky but adults seem to see things in a different light. My tongue is always getting me into trouble. It all began, the trouble this evening, when I was fidgeting in the armchair; I was not interested in the play my parents were watching. I made critical remarks and was sharply told, 'We're listening to the play, not you.' I got up and walked towards the door; 'Where are you going?' It was always the same, wherever I went I was asked the same question. Why couldn't they leave me alone? I felt a surge of resentment. I came back and stood in front of the fireplace. I was then told gruffly, 'You're blocking Nanny's view.'

'If she can't see, she should say so and not wait for someone else to do it.' There! I had said it, it just slipped out before I knew it. My mother sat forward in her chair. Nobody was looking at the television now, all eyes were focussed on me. They were all eyeing me with dislike, probably thinking what a horrid girl I was. I was thinking the same about myself. If only I could take those words back, but I couldn't.

'Go to bed,' said my father sternly.

'But it's only just gone ten,' I said rebelliously.

'Go to bed,' said my father, the tone of his voice developing into a shout. I went to the door. Without turning I said 'goodnight' to them; I usually kissed them, but not tonight. I felt the tears well up inside me, my nose tingling as I tried hard to fight back the tears.

'Haven't we got names?' said my father.

'Goodnight Nan, goodnight Dad, goodnight Mum,' I said shortly as if reading a list. Then I went from the room, banging the door behind me.

In the bedroom I sat on the edge of my bed, shivering in the dark. I wanted to have a good cry but the tears would not come. I turned my bedside lamp on and got into bed. With a faint smile I remembered I had some sweets under my pillow. Things to eat always gave me comfort when I was in trouble. I said my prayers; this usually comforted me, but at the moment I felt that He would not want to listen to a horrid girl like me. My mother has often said 'Never let the sun go down on your anger.' But I was too proud to go and apologise so I went to sleep unsettled and I knew tomorrow would start badly too. I sighed, hardly a day went by without having an argument.

'Oh God, please make me less argumentative and help me to curb my quick temper and my tongue.'

Prayer

We get angry too quickly, lose our tempers and then people get angry with us. We need your help to understand ourselves. Sometimes we think we know all the answers but we do really need to appreciate the help that other people give to us, and to do that, we need you.

In The Beginning

Music

'All things Bright and Beautiful' played by Joe Brown (Pye GH 583)

Reading

'Genesis' by Brian Morris

'Who are you?' said the Prime Minister, opening the door.

'I am God,' replied the stranger.

'I don't believe you,' sneered the Prime Minister. 'Show me a miracle.'

And God showed the Prime Minister the miracle of birth.

'Pah,' said the Prime Minister. 'My scientists are creating life in test tubes and have nearly solved the secret of heredity. Artificial in-semination is more certain than your lackadaisical method, and by cross-breeding we are producing fish and mammals to our design. Show me a proper miracle.'

And God caused the sky to darken and hailstones came pouring down.

'That's nothing,' said the Prime Minister, picking up the telephone to the Air Ministry. 'Send up a met. plane would you, old chap, and sprinkle the clouds with silver chloride crystals.'

And the met. plane went up and sprinkled the clouds which had darkened the world and the hailstones stopped pouring down and the sun shone brightly.

'Show me another,' said the Prime Minister.

And God caused a plague of frogs to descend upon the land.

The Prime Minister picked up his telephone. 'Get the Min. of Ag. and Fish,' he said to the operator, 'and instruct them to procure a frog-killer as myxomatosis killed rabbits.'

And soon the land was free of frogs, and the people gave thanks to the Prime Minister and erected laboratories in his name.

'Show me another,' sneered the Prime Minister.

And God caused the sea to divide.

The Prime Minister picked up his direct-link-telephone to the Polaris submarine.

'Lob a few ICBMs into Antarctica and melt the ice-cap, please, old man.'

And the ice-cap melted into water and the sea came rushing back.

'I will kill all the first-born,' said God.

'Paltry tricks,' said the Prime Minister. 'Watch this.' He pressed a button on his desk. And missiles flew to their pre-ordained destinations and H-bombs split the world asunder and radio-activity killed every mortal thing.

'I can raise the dead,' said God.

'Please,' said the Prime Minister in his cardboard coffin. 'Let me live again.'

'Why, who are you?' said God, closing the lid.

Prayer

From James, aged five years:
'You must take care of love
If you don't, it goes bad...'

Mothers

Music

'Song of the Seashore' played by James Galway
(*from* Song of the Seashore: RCA RK 25253)

Reading

'. . . And God Created Mothers' by Erma Bombeck

When the good Lord was creating mothers, he was into his sixth day of overtime when an angel appeared and said, 'You're doing a lot of fiddling around on this one.'

And the Lord said, 'Have you read the specifications on this order? She has to be completely washable, but not plastic. . .have 180 movable parts – all replaceable. . .run on black coffee and leftovers. . . have a lap that disappears when she stands up. . .a kiss that can cure anything from a broken leg to a disappointed love affair. . .and six pairs of hands.'

The angel shook her head slowly and said, 'Six pairs of hands? No way.'

'It's not the hands that are causing me problems,' said the Lord. 'It's the three pairs of eyes that mothers have to have.'

'That's on the standard model?' asked the angel.

The Lord nodded. 'One pair that sees through closed doors when she asks, "What are you children doing in there?" when she already knows. Another in the back of head that sees what she shouldn't but what she has to know. And, of course, the ones in front that can look at a child when he gets himself into trouble and say 'I understand and I love you' without so much as uttering a word.'

'Lord,' said the angel, touching his sleeve gently, 'go to bed. Tomorrow is another. . .'

'I can't,' said the Lord. 'I'm so close now. Already I have one who heals herself when she is sick, can feed a family of six on one pound of mince, and can get a nine-year-old to have a bath.'

The angel circled the model of a mother very slowly. 'It's too soft,' she sighed.

'But tough!' said the Lord excitedly. 'You cannot imagine what this mother can do or endure.'

'Can it think?'

'Not only think, but it can reason and compromise,' said the Creator.

Finally the angel bent over and ran her finger across the cheek.

'There's a leak,' she pronounced.

'It's not a leak,' said the Lord. 'It's a tear.'
'What's it for?'
'It's for joy, sadness, disappointment, pain, loneliness and pride.'
'You are a genius,' said the angel.
The Lord looked sombre. 'I didn't put it there.'

Prayer

In our busy days we often take for granted the
love and kindness of our parents. If we are
lacking in understanding and care, help us to
think and to see.
In a moment of quiet, let us all think our own
thoughts...

Varied Talents
(A different view of harvest)

Music

*'All Good Gifts Around Us' from the original London cast
recording of* Godspell *(Bell ZC BEL 203)*

Reading

'My Son, the Carpenter' by Richard Bode

Five years ago, a friend asked me where my eldest son was going to college. 'Jeff's not going to college,' I replied. 'He wants to be a carpenter.'

I knew that my friend's son had been accepted as a medical student by a prestigious university. The proud father had often jokingly referred to his boy as my son, the doctor.' Clearly embarrassed now, my friend mumbled, 'How nice!' and changed the subject. It was obvious he thought my son should put aside his silly notion and go to college. Indeed, I had often vigorously expressed the same opinion.

I had always assumed that all my children would go to college. So my wife and I did everything possible to prepare our offspring for higher education, reading to them as children and exposing them to art. I tried to get Jeff interested in economics. I urged him to apply himself to maths, certain he had the makings of a first-rate civil engineer.

I was wrong. The quality of Jeff's intelligence was quite different from mine. He wasn't interested in abstractions but had his own practical turn of mind, which I chose to ignore. While I thought with my head, he seemed to think with his hands. In my bias, I believed his way of thinking was inferior.

Yet he often showed me how inadequate I was. On camping trips, his innate handiness saved me from disaster many a time. My wife said that if she were stranded on a desert island, she would rather have Jeff there than me. He would build a shelter and a roaring fire while I fumed about my bad luck.

Jeff's mechanical aptitudes surfaced early in may ways. When he was nine, I purchased a picnic table and brought the pieces home in a big box. While I pored over the instructions, he assembled the table. We still use it.

At ten, he began to tie and sell intricate freshwater fishing flies. He made regular trips to the local furrier for scraps of discarded rabbit or mink fur. I still see those flies in his tackle box, and I realize how essential they were to the educational process that suited him.

But, at the time, I told my wife there was no place in industrial society for a latter-day Robinson Crusoe. I said a youngster had to go to college to be educated to take his place in a specialized world.

But Jeff was determined to become a carpenter, and when he left school he started to contact building firms. One local contractor kept telling him to 'come back next week'. Jeff persisted. Then, one August day, he burst into the house at noon to grab a sandwich. 'They took me on!' he shouted. 'I'm building a house! I'm an apprentice carpenter.'

With a sudden sense of identify, Jeff matured. The boy who couldn't get out of bed in the mornings was out of the house by 7.15 a.m. He learned his trade and earned his keep. He found out how to handle money and how to work with others. Eventually, he became a journeyman carpenter.

He also learned about the ups and downs. No sooner did he become a journeyman than the recession put him out of work. He collected unemployment pay only as long as it took him to pack off to where he *could* find work. Now he's home again, working. He eventually hopes to run his own business as a builder.

Jeff's course is hardly for everyone. I still hope he will broaden his education, take a deeper interest in those academic subjects we call 'humanities'. If he does, they may mean more to him because of his own direct encounter with life.

A few years ago, he built a huge sun porch behind our house. On summer evenings, the family gathers there, and I look around and admire the lap-jointed frames and door, the snug moulding and sturdy rails.

The whole design came out of Jeff's mind. I say to myself with pride: 'Yes, this was built by my son, the carpenter.'

Prayer

All good gifts around us are
Sent from Heaven above.
Then thank the Lord, O thank the Lord,
For all his love.

Easter

Music

'Cavatina' by John Williams (from Changes: *Cube Tapes KT OF2 8065)*

Reading

One Solitary Life (Anonymous — quoted in The Presidio)

Here is a young man who was born in an obscure village, the child of a peasant woman. He grew up in another village. He worked in a carpenter's shop until he was thirty, and then for three years he was an itinerant preacher. He never wrote a book. He never held office. He never owned a home. He never had a family. He never went to college. He never put his foot inside a big city. He never travelled 200 miles from the place where he was born. He never did one of the things that usually accompany greatness. He had no credentials but himself.

While he was still a young man, the tide of public opinion turned against him. His friends ran away. He was turned over to his enemies. He went through the mockery of a trial. He was nailed to a cross between two thieves. While he was dying, his executioners gambled for the only piece of property he had on earth, that was his coat. When he was dead, he was laid in a borrowed grave through the pity of a friend.

Music

'Cavatina' or 'Were you there when they crucified my Lord?'
(sung by the children)

Nineteen centuries have passed, and today he is the central figure of the human race and leader of the column of progress.

I am far within the mark when I say that all the armies that ever marched, and all the navies that were ever built, and all the parliaments that ever sat, and all the kings that ever reigned, put together, have not affected the life of man upon this earth as has that one solitary life.

Music

As above

Prayer

Thank you for the life of Jesus Christ.
Help us to be generous and self-giving.
May we see you more clearly, follow you
more nearly and love you more dearly, day
by day...

On a Winter's Morning

Music

'Snowflakes Are Dancing' by Debussy, arranged by Tomita
(from Tomita's Greatest Hits: RCA RK 43076)

Reading

'Isn't it Lovely?' by Tony Winter

The snow fell, bitter and chill, but from the warm house it looked clean and beautiful. It spun down drifting reluctantly in tiny particles to the ground, smoothing everything out like white icing on a cake.

Jim looked out of his window. He had a paper round to do, and, seeing the falling snow, he decided to wear his duffle coat. He had been out in the snow before, but only for fun and when he became cold he had gone indoors again. Today was different, but as he started across the street he noticed how beautiful was the falling snow. It seemed to be attracted to the street lights that made it stand out brightly against the sky, shimmering gloriously. What Jim did not know was how deceptively fierce it was; but it seemed rather soft and gentle when he watched it. He was even looking forward to being the first to tread in the pure, crisp snow. Then he went downstairs and he stepped out into the snow and he was rudely awakened! The snow was not calm and gentle. It was harshly cold! He thought how it seemed to fall so softly when viewed from indoors and yet when outside it splattered him in a cruel attack, and bit at his face. The snow was still the same in one respect – inside or out, it fell in quiet serenity.

As he scrunched through the snow, his imagination wandered. He thought of himself as a famous explorer trudging his way through an Arctic blizzard. Then his old enemy, the dog at number 72 appeared and stood barking at him. The shaggy white dog stood, oblivious to the cold, and Jim's imagination converted it into a polar bear and he, the brave explorer, advanced slowly. Then the bear-hound retreated so there was no need for Jim to shoot it after all. So, he continued his journey to the Arctic laboratory – known as Squibo's Shop. Then he crossed the footbridge – which he imagined was a deep crevice – and he went into the newsagents.

When he came out again, he soon forgot about the exploring game. The snow was thicker and it soaked his gloves. If he took them off his hands would get cold, yet the wet gloves numbed his fingers with chill when he kept them on. Then, as he walked down the street he saw an ambulance outside one of the houses. He asked the driver, just getting back into the ambulance, who was ill.

'Old Mrs Jones has died of hypothermia,' replied the driver glumly, and they both fell silent. Jim just stood. The atmosphere grew tense, so tense that Jim could do nothing but walk off without saying anything more.

Jim felt stunned – as though it were Saturday evening and Monday morning all at the same time. He had lost concentration and posted a paper into number 59 but realized that the family living there had moved a few days ago and he had posted the paper for number 63 there by mistake. A mistake that would cost him the price of a *Daily Telegraph*.

The wind got up again and he continued his round, but it was becoming difficult. His nose went red, so he breathed through his mouth, but the snow made his teeth feel like icicles. His shoes became soaked and his feet became nearly as cold as his hands. The newspapers became soggy and wet and some ripped as he pushed them through the letterboxes. He bent down to tie his shoe-lace, and his scarf draped in the snow, absorbing water like a sponge. He could not see the ground beneath him and he tripped on the kerb when delivering the paper to number 38. In the end, he made it home and he was a tired, bedraggled paperboy who exchanged his wet clothes for his school uniform. When he went downstairs again, his Mother asked him to go and make sure his little brother was rising. When he entered the bedroom his little brother was awake already and drawing the curtains. Jim disagreed with him as he exclaimed: 'Look at the snow! Isn't it lovely?'

Prayer

Bless all our work today. May all we do be our *very best*.

He's Not Tough, He's Gentle

Music

'Annie's Song' played by James Galway (from Songs for Annie:
RCA RK/RL 70257)

Reading

from An Episode of Sparrows *by Rumer Godden*

*Lovejoy Mason is a lonely little girl who has made a garden on a
sheltered corner of a bomb site.*

Tip's camp was the best hidden for miles; screened by a bit of an old
wall, it was like an igloo built of rubble; there was only a little hole,
close to the ground, by which to go in and out; even the smallest of
the boys had to lie down and wriggle. Outside it looked just another
pile of bricks and stones; inside it had bunks made of orange boxes,
an old meat-safe for keeping things in and an older cooking-stove in
which it was possible to light a fire or heat up a sausage or soup over
a candle; drinks were kept in a hot-water bottle...

The gang had thought it completely secret but 'She's there now,'
said Sparkey breathlessly. 'I just seen her go in.'

The next moment they were through the gap, down the bank and
in the bomb-ruin. There was a violent noise of boots on stones, of
hoots and cries as they hunted among the walls, then they found her
and Lovejoy was surrounded.

One minute the garden was there, its stones arranged, the corn-
flowers growing, the grass green, the next there were only boots. To
Lovejoy they were boots, though most of the boys wore shoes, but
boys' shoes with heavy steel tips to the soles and heels. She crouched
where she was, while the boys smashed up the garden, trampled
down the grass and kicked away the stones; the cornflower earth was
scattered, the seedlings torn out and pulled in bits. In a minute no
garden was left, and Tip picked up the trowel and fork and threw
them far away cross the ruble. 'Now get out,' said Tip to Lovejoy.

Lovejoy stood up; she felt as if she were made of stone, she was so
cold and hard, then, in a boy's hand she saw an infinitesimal bit of
green; he was rolling a cornflower between his finger and thumb;
suddenly her chin began to tremble...

Tip had seen two things the other boys had not. He had seen the
garden as a whole – a vision of something laid out, green and alive,
carefully edged with stones; the other thing he had seen, and saw
now, only he did not want to look was the trembling of Lovejoy's

chin. She had not uttered a sound, not screamed. Tip connected females with screams and cries and here was only this small trembling. It made him feel uncomfortable...

'Get out,' he said to Lovejoy but less fiercely. As she still seemed dazed he put his hand on her shoulder to turn her...she turned her head, bit Tip's hand, and ran.

It was an hour or two later that Cassie burst into the Masons' room. She never knocked. One does not knock for children.

'There's a boy wants to see you,' she told Lovejoy.

'I don't want to see a boy,' said Lovejoy.

'Don't you feel well?' asked curious Cassie.

'Quite well,' said Lovejoy but she felt neither well nor ill; she felt nothing, nothing at all; she might have been dead. 'You can come down or go to bed,' said Cassie.

Lovejoy came down... Her fingers gripped in her pocket and found the pill-box. Thoughtfully she took it outside and emptied it... Lovejoy was thinking wearily, when a boy came up from the shadow by the side door. It was Tip.

Lovejoy stiffened. 'What do you want?' she asked, backing against the house wall.

'I came to bring you this,' he said and held out the garden fork. 'I couldn't find the trowel,' said Tip, 'but we've got a little shovel...'

Lovejoy made no attempt to hold the fork; as she walked away to the edge of the pavement she let it drop from her hand into the gutter; then she sat down on the kerb and began to cry.

Tip was one of those boys who are so big and strong that people do not really look at them; they look at their boots, their big young knees and shoulders, their jaws perhaps, but not at them. 'What a young tough!' people said of Tip, but Mrs Malone, who knew him better than anyone else, said, 'He's not tough. He's gentle.' Few people divined this. Yet Lovejoy divined it, at once.

To Lovejoy, Tip was a bitter-enemy boy, the biggest and worst of the ones who had smashed her garden, and yet she, who never cried in front of anyone, who had not cried then, was moved to cry now, in front of him. He did not jeer at her, nor did he go away embarrassed; he picked up the fork and sat down on the kerb beside her.

Prayer

When we have to mix with people we fear or do not like, help us to remember that they are your creation, and that everyone will eventually respond to love and gentleness. When we find ourselves in difficult situations, help us to remember we can always call upon you for help.

To the Top of the Mountain

Music

Gymnopedie No. I by Satie, arranged by John Williams, and played by Sky (Ariola ZC/ARL 5022)

Reading

from Change Lobsters and Dance *by Lilli Palmer*

In the summer of 1950, my husband and I were living in a house built high above Portofino in Italy. The view was extraordinary. Far below us on the right lay the blue harbour, with its romantic peninsula and the old castle. To our left was the tiny emerald bay of Paraggi, with its white beach framed by cypresses.

There was, however, a serpent in our paradise: the path up the cliff to our house. The municipal authorities had refused us permission to build a proper road instead of the mule track. The only vehicle we had that could climb the narrow path and negotiate the hairpin bends, steep incline and potholes was an old American Army Jeep.

One day, Contessa Margot Besozzi, who lived higher up our path, called to say that her cousin had arrived at Portofino with a companion and that her own Jeep had broken down. Would I mind going down to the Hotel Splendido to fetch the two old ladies in ours?

'Just ask for Miss Helen Keller,' she said.

'Margot,' I gasped. 'You don't mean Helen Keller?'

'Of course,' she replied. 'She's my cousin. Didn't you know?'

I ran to our garage, jumped into the Jeep and bounced down the mountain.

I had been twelve years old when my father gave me Helen Keller's autobiography to read. In that book she had written of Anne Sullivan, the remarkable woman whom fate had chosen to be the teacher of the blind and deaf child. Miss Sullivan had turned the rebellious, brutish little creature into a civilized member of society by teaching her to speak.

I still remembered vividly her description of the first weeks of physical battle with the child, until the glorious moment when, holding Helen's hand under running water at the pump, she spelt w-a-t-e-r into the other hand, and the mystery of language was revealed to the transfixed little girl.

When I backed the Jeep against a flower-covered wall and presented myself at the hotel, a tall, buxom woman rose from a chair on the terrace to greet me: Polly Thomson, Helen Keller's companion. A second figure rose slowly from the chair beside her and held out her hand. Helen Keller, then in her seventies, was a slight, white-haired woman with wide-open blue eyes and a shy smile.

'How do you do?' she said slowly and a little gutturally. I took her hand, which she was holding too high because she didn't know how tall I was. She was bound to make this mistake with people she was meeting for the first time, but she never made it twice. Later, when we said good-bye, she put her hand firmly into mine at exactly the right level.

The luggage was loaded into the back of the Jeep, and I helped the jolly Miss Thomson to her seat beside it.

At the foot of the rocky path, I stopped the Jeep, turned to her and said, 'Miss Keller, we're going to go up a very steep hill. Can you hold tight to this metal on the windscreen?'

She continued to look expectantly straight ahead. Behind me, Miss Thomson said patiently, 'She can't hear you, dear, or see you. I know it's hard to get used to it at first.'

I was so embarrassed that I stammered like an idiot, trying to explain the problem ahead of us. Miss Thomson knelt across the luggage and reached for Miss Keller's hand. Rapidly she moved Helen's fingers up, down and sideways, telling her in blind-deaf language what I had just said.

'I don't mind,' said Helen, laughing. 'I'll hold tight.'

I placed her hands on the piece of metal in front of her. 'OK,' Helen cried gaily. The Jeep started off with a jump, and Miss Thomson fell off her seat onto the luggage. I couldn't stop because of the steep trail and unreliable brakes. We roared upwards, with Miss Thomson as helpless as a beetle on its back.

Helen Keller was the first passenger who was oblivious to the dangers of the precipitous drops and hairpin bends.

She actually began to sing. 'This is fun,' she warbled happily, bouncing up and down. 'Lovely!' she cried. She was enjoying the crazy ride like a child riding up and down on a wooden horse on a merry-go-round.

At last, we rounded the final curve between two giant fig trees, and I could see Margot Besozzi and her husband waiting for us. Helen was lifted out of the Jeep and hugged; the luggage was unloaded, Polly Thomson was upended and dusted down.

While the two old women were being shown to their rooms, Margot told me about her cousin and her life. 'All she really notices,' Margot said, 'is a change of smell. Whether she's here or in New York or in India, she sits in a black, silent hole.'

Arm in arm, casually, as if they just happened to be fond of each other, Helen and Polly walked through the garden towards the terrace, where we were waiting for them. 'That must be wistaria,' said Helen, 'and masses of it, too. I recognize the scent.'

Helen's diction was not quite normal. She spoke haltingly, like someone who has had a stroke, and her consonants were slow and laboured. She turned to me, looking directly at me because she had sensed where I was sitting. 'You know, we're on the way to Florence to see Michelangelo's David. I'm so thrilled. I've always wanted to see it.'

Mystified, I looked at Miss Thomson, who nodded. 'It's true,' she said. 'The Italian government has had scaffolding erected round the statue so that Helen can climb up and touch it. That's what she calls "seeing". We often go to the theatre, and I tell her what's going on onstage and describe the actors. Sometimes we go backstage, too, so that she can "see" the sets and the actors. Then she goes home, feeling that she's really witnessed the performance.'

Luncheon was served. Helen was led to her chair, and I watched her 'see' her place setting. Quickly, her hands moved over the objects on the table – plate, glass, silverware – memorizing where they were. Never during the meal did she grope about, but reached out casually and firmly like the rest of us. Whatever suffering must have tormented her – and might still torment her – her face showed no trace of it. It was an isolated face, a saintly face.

Through her friend, I asked her what else she wanted to see in Europe. She slowly mapped out her journey – all the places she would visit and the people she would meet. Incredibly, she spoke French quite well and could make herself understood in German and Italian. 'There's still so much I'd like to see,' she said, 'so much to learn. And death is just around the corner. Not that that worries me. On the contrary.'

'Do you believe in life after death?' I asked.

'Most certainly,' she said emphatically. 'It is no more than passing from one room into another.'

We sat in silence for a moment. Then, slowly and very distinctly, she spoke again: 'But there's a difference for me, you know. Because in that other – room – I shall be able to see.'

Prayer

Thank you for this new day, with its hopes and opportunities. Help us all to appreciate the beauty of nature. Guide us to be childlike but not childish...

A Piece of Bread

Music

Air on the G String by Bach, arranged by Eugene Ormandy
(from Commercial Break: CBS *Classics #40–61836)*

Reading

'The Heart of a Child' by Marius Barnard

All his short life the world had failed him. Now Saul had one last wish.

It was seven o'clock on a Wednesday night when I met Saul, the last patient on my round of Cape Town's Groote Schuur Hospital. A small, frightened figure, he was to undergo open-heart surgery the next morning.

Although he was sixteen-years-old, Saul weighed less than five stone. He was short of breath, his body and liver were swollen, his heartbeat was abnormally fast and irregular.

When I greeted Saul, he smiled back, eyes bright and hopeful, and for a moment anxiety left his face. He was one of eight children in a desperately poor family. They lived in a *pondokkie*, one of the thousands of wood and iron shacks on the wind-blown Cape Flats.

All his life, Saul had known only sickness. As a toddler he had contracted rheumatic fever, the cause of his diseased heart and shrivelled body. Schooling had been limited, and he had been unable to play games with other children. His clothes were hand-me-downs, toys something that existed in another world, and ice-creams had never touched his lips. At night he shared his bed with his brothers and sisters. Mealtimes all too often found his mother with nothing to offer the children but bread.

Next morning, I saw Saul on the operating table, anaesthetized and ready for the five-hour operation to replace the diseased mitral valve in his heart. We started our task with barely a word spoken.

When the task was completed, Saul's heart took over its own function with a regular beat and pressure was good. His chest was closed and Saul was returned to the intensive care unit in a satisfactory condition. We expected no special problems.

That night, though, Saul's blood pressure dropped and his circulation deteriorated. After further examination, it became clear that the only hope was to replace the other two diseased valves in his heart.

I went to Saul to explain as gently as I could that he would have to undergo another operation. A tube inserted through his mouth into his windpipe to help him breathe prevented him from talking. Splints, to keep in place the plastic tubes supplying fluid nutrients and antibiotics to his veins and monitoring the vital functions, restricted movement of his arms.

I smiled and turned to the operating theatre. Something stopped me and I walked back to his bedside. I leaned over and asked quietly: 'Wil jy iets se, Saul?' – 'Do you want to say something?' The boy nodded. A nurse brought a piece of paper and a pencil and, in scratchy, almost illegible writing, Saul scrawled his simple request: stukkie brood – a piece of bread.

I stood still. In the midst of his discomfort and fear, and the realization that he had to undergo another operation, the boy wanted the reassurance of the one comfort he knew – just a piece of bread. 'It's not possible, Saul,' I whispered in Afrikaans. 'You cannot eat before an operation. Afterwards there will be plenty of bread.'

Saul's condition was now critical. For his first operation he had been anaesthetized in the ante-room. Now there was no time. I was already scrubbed and gowned when he was wheeled into the operating theatre. His eyes widened as they took in the strange sights that now confronted him; white sterile tiles, big overhead lights, weird shiny machinery, masked strangers in green surgical gowns.

The team went to work quickly, efficiently. His heart was re-opened, his blood-stream again connected to the heart-lung machine. We then carried out the necessary surgery in his heart. Then, it was up to Saul's own heart to take over its vital functions. The heart was sewn up, a final check made for any significant bleeding, and the time came for the by-pass machine to be disconnected. 'Switch off the pump,' I said confidently.

Immediately, Saul's heart rate slowed and his blood pressure dropped. Switching the artificial pump on again, we administered drugs to improve the heartbeat.

A second time I ordered the pump to be stopped. Once again his heartbeat weakened and his blood pressure dropped ominously. The pump was restarted, and we tried everything possible to improve his heart action.

Ten minutes later, a third attempt failed.

We fought for another half-hour. The pump went off and on, off and on. Each time Saul's heart failed to pick up its own lifebeat. I could see in the eyes of the others round the table that they knew, as I did, that the time was coming when I would not order the pump to be restarted. The moment of failure.

We tried once more. Then, finally, 'Pump off.' The heart beat weakly. Gradually the blood pressure dropped. Minutes later, after a few more weak, futile, irregular beats, Saul's heart stopped.

The theatre was quiet. I turned away and wearily removed my gown, mask and cap. I wanted to say something. But all I could think about was Saul. He had known only poverty, overcrowding, sickness. He was brought to a modern hospital where he was tended by people who had trained long and intensively in their field. He was operated on with expensive, complex equipment, and valves worth hundreds of pounds had been placed in his heart.

In short, we had given him the very best in knowledge and technique that our sophisticated medical world had to offer. Yet, we'd failed to fulfil his one simple comforting need: a piece of bread.

Prayer

Bow your heads, close your eyes and consider what you have just heard as the music is playing.

Music

Fade up 'Air on the G String'

They Too Have Their Place

Music

*'Memories of Summer' by Tony Hatch played by the Tony Hatch Orchestra
(from* Mr Nice Guy: *Golden Hour ZCGH 628)*

Reading

'Our Secret'
'Some Other Day'   *(both poems from* The Reader's Digest)

'Our Secret'

Hey, Lord, we have a secret.
There are some things about being old that are fun.
Yes, fun.
The world gets off your back.
They neglect you.
You don't have to keep up appearances.
So you can go back to the fun of being a child.
Watching a spider spin a web.
Making shadow pictures against the light.
Exploring the garden as if it were a new country.
Eating apple sauce and cream instead of dinner.
Dawdling.
Staying up all night. Counting stars.
Staying home from a dull party to play chess with an old friend.
Wearing a funny hat.
Why didn't You tell me that besides all the things I hate
  about being old, there'd be some fun in it too?
I know, I know.
I wouldn't have believed You.

Music

Fade up Memories of Summer

Reading

'Some Other Day'

Preserve me from the occupational therapist, God.
She means well, but I'm too busy to make baskets.
I want to re-live a day in July
When Sam and I went berry-picking.
I was eighteen,

My hair was long and thick
And I braided it and wound it round my head so it wouldn't get
    caught on the briars.
But when we sat down in the shade to rest
I unpinned it and it came tumbling down,
And Sam proposed.
I suppose it wasn't fair
To use my hair to make him fall in love with me,
But it turned out a good marriage...
Oh, here she comes, the therapist, with scissors and paste.
Would I like to try a découpage?
'No,' I say, 'I haven't got time.'
That's not what I mean,
I mean that all my life I've been doing things
For people, with people. I have to catch up
On my thinking and feeling.
About Sam's death, for one thing.
Close to the end, I asked if there was anything I could do...
He said, 'Yes, unpin your hair.'
I said, 'Oh, Sam, it's so thin now and grey.'
'Please,' he said, 'unpin it anyway.'
I did and he reached out his hand –
The skin transparent, I could see the blue veins –
And stroked my hair.
If I close my eyes, I can feel it, Sam.
'Please open your eyes,' the therapist says;
'You don't want to sleep the day away.'
She wants to know what I used to do,
Knit? Crochet?
Yes, I did those things,
And cooked and cleaned
And reared five children,
And had things happen to me.
Beautiful things, terrible things,
I need to think about them,
Arrange them on the shelves of my mind.
The therapist is showing me glittery beads.
She asks if I might like to make jewellery.
She's a dear child and means well,
So I tell her I might.
Some other day.

Music

As above

Prayer

Hard though it may be,
Help us to understand and to care,
To be aware and to be sensitive...

Winter Time

Music

In the Bleak Midwinter (as a sung hymn or pre-recorded)

Reading

'Christmas Landscape' from The Bloom of Candles *by Laurie Lee*

Tonight the wind gnaws
with teeth of glass,
the jackdaw shivers
in caged branches of iron,
the stars have talons.

There is hunger in the mouth
of vole and badger,
silver agonies of breath
in the nostrils of the fox,
ice on the rabbit's paw.

Tonight has no moon,
no food for the pilgrim;
the fruit tree is bare,
the rose bush a thorn
and the ground bitter with stones.

But the mole sleeps, and the hedgehog
lies curled in a womb of leaves,
the beans and the wheat seed
hug their germs in the earth
and the stream moves under the ice.

Tonight there is no moon,
but a new star opens
like a silver trumpet over the dead.
Tonight in a nest of ruins
the blessed babe is laid.

And the fir tree warms to a bloom of candles,
the child lights his lantern,
stares at his tinselled toy;
our hearts and hearths
smoulder with live ashes.

In the blood of our grief
the cold earth is suckled,
in our agony the womb
convulses its seed,
in the cry of anguish
the child's first breath is born.

Prayer

We know that some truths are beyond our understanding
and the universe is filled with secrets. Teach us
understanding and help us to nurture the love and
truth that was born in a stable long ago...

Christmas

Music

'Christmas Song' by Gilbert O'Sullivan
(MAM Records Ltd ZX DR 56658 MAM 124)

Reading

'Albert's Christmas Ship' by Keith Waterhouse

Below the military striking clock in the City Arcade there was, and for all I know, still is, a fabulous toyshop, the nearest thing on this earth to Santa's Workshop.

Once a year, at Christmas-time, everybody who was anybody was taken to see the clock strike noon – an event in our lives as colourful and as immovable in the calendar of pageantry as the Trooping the Colour. Even Albert Skinner, whose father never took him anywhere, not even to the Education Office to explain why he'd been playing truant, somehow tagged on like a stray dog. And after the mechanical soldiers of the King had trundled back into their plaster-of-Paris garrison, he, with the rest of us, was allowed to press his nose to the toyshop window.

Following a suitable period of meditation, we were conveyed home on the rattling tram. And there, thawing out our mottled legs by the fireside, we were supposed to compose our petitions to Father Christmas.

With our blank jotters on our knees, we would suck our copying-ink pencils until our tongues turned purple. It wasn't that we were short of ideas. Far from it; there was too much choice. For the fabulous toy-shop was like a bankruptcy sale in heaven. There was a big clockwork train and a small electric train, and Noah's Ark, and a tram conductor's set, and a small cycle, and a tin steam-roller, and annuals, and board games, and chemistry sets, and conjuring sets. And as the centrepiece of the window display there was always something out of the reach of ordinary mortals: the Blackpool Tower in Meccano, or a mechanical carousel with horses that went up and down on their brass poles, or Windsor Castle made of a million building bricks.

This year the window featured a splendid model of the *Queen Mary*, which had been recently launched on Clydebank. It was about four feet long, with real lights in the portholes, real steam curling out of the funnels, and passengers, and lifeboats, all to scale – clearly it was not for the likes of us. Having marvelled at it, we dismissed this expensive dream from our minds and settled down to list our requests for Plasticine, farmyard animals that poisoned you when you licked the paint off, or one pair of roller skates between two of us.

All of us, that is, except Albert Skinner, who calmly announced that he was asking Father Christmas for the *Queen Mary*.

This, as you might imagine, was greeted with some scepticism.

'You've never asked for that, have you? You're having us on.'

'I'm not – God's honour.'

'What else have you asked for?'

'Nowt. I don't want owt else. I just want the *Queen Mary*. And I'm getting it, as well.'

Little else was said at the time, but privately we thought Albert was a bit of an optimist. For one thing, the *Queen Mary* was so big and so grand and so lit-up that it was probably not even for sale. For another, we were all well aware that Father Christmas's representative in the Skinner household was a sullen, foul-tempered collier who also happened to be unemployed. Albert's birthday present, it was generally known, had been a pair of boots – instead of the scooter he had set his heart on.

Even so, Albert continued to insist that he was getting the *Queen Mary* for Christmas. 'Ask my dad,' he would say. 'If you don't believe me, ask my dad.'

None of us cared to broach the subject with the excitable Mr Skinner. But sometimes, when we went to his house to swop comics, Albert would raise the matter himself. 'Dad, I am, aren't I? Getting that *Queen Mary* for Christmas?'

Mr Skinner, dourly whittling a piece of wood by the fireside after the habit of all the local miners, would growl without looking up: 'You'll get a clout over the bloomin' earhole if you don't stop nattering.'

Albert would turn to us complacently. 'I am, see. I'm getting the *Queen Mary*'.

Sometimes, when his father had come home from the pub in a bad mood (which was quite often), Albert's pleas for reassurance would meet with a more vicious response. 'You gormless little git, will you shut up about the *Queen Mary*!' Mr Skinner would shout. 'If I hear one more word about it, you'll get *nothing* for Christmas!'

Outside, his ear tingling from the blow his father had landed on it, Albert would bite back the tears and declare stubbornly: 'I'm still getting it. You just wait.'

Then one day the crippled lad at No. 43 was taken to see the military striking clock, and when he came home he reported that the *Queen Mary* was no longer in the toyshop window. 'I know,' said Albert, having confirmed that his father was out of earshot. 'I'm getting it for Christmas.'

And, indeed, it seemed the only explanation possible. The fabulous toyshop never changed its glittering display until after Boxing Day; never. And yet the *Queen Mary* had gone. Had Father Christmas gone mad? Had Mr Skinner bribed him – and if so, with what? Had Mr Skinner won the football pools? Or was it that Albert's unswerving faith could move mountains – not to mention ocean-going liners with real steam and real lights in the portholes? Or was it, as one cynic among us insisted, that the *Queen Mary* had been privately purchased for some pampered grammar-school boy on the posher side of town?

'You just wait and see,' said Albert.

Then it was Christmas morning, and we all flocked out to show off our presents, sucking our brand new torches to make our cheeks glow red, or brandishing a lead soldier or two in the pretence that we had a whole regiment of them indoors. There was no sign of Albert. No one, in fact, expected to see him at all. But just as we were asking each other what Father Christmas could have brought him – a new jersey, perhaps, or a balaclava helmet – he came bounding, leaping, almost somersaulting into the street. 'I've got it! I've got it!'

Toys and games abandoned in the gutter, we clustered round Albert, who was cradling in his arms what seemed on first inspection to be a length of wood. Then we saw that it had been carved at both ends to make a bow and stern, and that three cotton reels had been nailed to it for funnels. A row of tin-tacks marked the Plimsoll line, and there were stuck-on bits of card-board for the portholes. The whole thing was painted in sticky lampblack, except for the wobbling white lettering on the port side. *The Queen Mary*, it said.

'See!' crowed Albert, complacently. 'I told you he'd fetch me it, and he's fetched me it.'

Our grunts of appreciation were genuine enough. Albert's *Queen Mary* was a crude piece of work, but clearly many hours of labour, and much love, had gone into it. Its clumsy contours alone must have taken night after night of whittling by the fireside.

Mr Skinner, pyjama-jacket tucked into his trousers, had come out of the house and was standing by his garden gate. Albert, in a rush of happiness, flung his arms round his father and hugged him. Then he waved the *Queen Mary* on high.

'Look, Dad! Look what Father Christmas has fetched me! You knew he would, didn't you, all the time!'

'Get out of it, you soft little beggar,' said Mr Skinner, cuffing Albert over the head as a matter of habit before going indoors.

Prayer

Now close your eyes and think about the words of the song.

Music

Christmas song as before

You Are Like That

Music

'He's got the whole world in his hands' sung by Wanda Jackson
(from Portrait: *EMI/ST 21530)*

Reading

'Because You Are Like That' by R.H. Lloyd

The ship was steaming at full speed in the Gulf Stream one hundred miles off the coast of Florida under the command of Captain George H. Grant. The youngest member of the crew, a seventeen-year-old lad, had been sent by the chief mate to clear out the scuppers. He slipped and fell overboard, and no one saw the incident.

An hour later when the crew sat down to breakfast they noticed that the boy was not present. An immediate search was organised. Every inch of the ship was searched, but in vain. The Captain was informed. He summoned the chief mate on to the bridge and asked him when it was that he had last seen the boy. The chief mate replied that he had sent the lad to clear the starboard scupper at about 7.10 a.m.

Looking at his watch the captain noted that it read 8.21 a.m. An hour and eleven minutes had passed. In other words, the boy would be eighteen miles astern.

The captain without any hesitation ordered fuel oil to be pumped into the sea and kept the vessel on course for a few more minutes, until the oil had laid a path behind her. When the direction was well defined, the oil was shut off, the ship turned about and steamed back along the oil path exactly the way she had come.

'We have to go back twenty miles from here!' declared the captain, 'One hour and twenty minutes! Watch the time!'

The captain did not expect to find the boy. Cross winds and current cause drift, and a head is such a small object to spot in a vast area of rough seas. Besides which, he had been told that the boy could not swim.

He glanced at his watch. Only a few minutes to go.

'Reduce speed to slow,' he ordered.

His eyes kept sweeping to and fro, pausing here, pausing there.

Suddenly he gave the command, 'Stop the engines! Full astern! Stand by to get the boat away!'

Incredibly his uncanny knack of reading the sea had enabled him to spot the boy's head bobbing up and sinking down less than a hundred yards away. A rare feat of navigation coupled with years of experience had achieved the near impossible.

Later, when the boy had recovered from his ordeal, the captain went down to see him. In the course of the conversation he asked the boy:

'You couldn't swim and you were in the water for over two-and-a half hours. How did you ever manage to stay afloat?'

'Well sir,' he replied, 'I knew you would come back for me.'

'How could you be so sure that I would?' asked the captain.

The boy glanced up and said quietly, 'Because you are like that, sir.'

Prayer

May we be able to accept the help that others offer to us. May we see that others can do for us much that we cannot do for ourselves...

Loving, and Being Loved

Music

Theme from Love Story *from the original soundtrack recording*
(Paramount TC SPFL 267)

Reading

'Mother Often Annoyed Me' by Jenny Rees

Tomorrow, Mother's Day comes round again. It should be a quiet little celebration in the middle of our busy lives. But it won't be.

Mothers, by their very nature, don't seem to be the kind of people to trail quietness, exactly, in their wake. The reality of tomorrow will be anything but quiet.

In homes, all over the place, there will be the flurry of activity in the kitchen around breakfast time. Small hands and large masculine ones will be fussing around with tea-pots and laying out little arrangements on trays.

Some lucky mothers will get posies of flowers out of the garden.

Instead of the nice lie-in, mothers will be woken rather early by the sounds of excited anticipation. I know the feeling so well.

Tomorrow, my children will bring me their offerings. They'll be up with the dawn, thudding about in their room. They're old enough now, for me not to worry about them scalding themselves with the boiling water for tea – but I'll worry all the same.

Tomorrow, also, I shall miss my mother, who died five years ago. She was young, only 56.

She died of the cancer that had overshadowed her life for so long. She had brought up five children, loved and cared for us all and my impractical, cerebral father who couldn't change a lamp bulb, and was getting to the point where she could begin, at last, to live a life of her own.

But the blossoming of her middle years was tragically halted just as she was about to burst into flower.

I, then in my mid-thirties, had just begun to see her as she was to other people, to her many friends and others who were so attracted to her vitality.

Not long after she died, I met a stranger at a wedding. 'Are you Margie's daughter?' she asked. Yes, I said. 'I met her only once,' she went on.

'We were on the top of a bus going from Notting Hill Gate to Marble Arch. It was the most interesting bus ride of my life.'

Suddenly, I saw my mother as I hadn't been able to see her before.

I could only see her as she was in those last, difficult years.

She hung on so tenaciously. She gathered us around her, turning us all, wallowing about in our own problems of mortgages, marriages and small children, once more into her chickens.

Arriving at the hospital with books, letters, bunches of grapes and photographs of houses, children, dogs and cats, anxious to be the ones to do the giving, she would overwhelm us with what she gave back.

She did not leave us peacefully. She had to be dragged out of this world. No longer able to cook and iron and sew and tend her garden, she was reduced to words to set us her example.

'Look after them,' she instructed me. 'The only thing that is worth doing is loving people.'

It took months, even years, for it to sink in that we no longer had her to turn to. We were on our own in a way we'd never been alone before.

My little brother, the much-loved baby of the family, suffered in his particular way, too young to see that he would carry her around with him for ever.

Now, when he smiles I see my mother smiling.

But what I miss most is what I often thought would drive me round the bend: my mother's interference.

When the phone rings at 8.30 in the morning – not the time most people ring – I think it is her. I rush to the phone, already anticipating the feeling of irritation. What does she want now?

There is no one to replace her. There is just no one else who loved me like she did, in that particular loving way of hers. There is no one else who knows me as well as she did.

She was so sure, I remember, that I was never going to be able to cope without her. But her love, her love of life, had not gone with her. She'd left it all behind.

She, who thought I'd never cope, has given me what I needed to cope. She, herself, has filled that great gaping hole I thought I'd never be able to fill.

Prayer

Lord in this moment of stillness
Help me to remember that I am loved
Even though I don't deserve it.
I am loved by family and friends
And amazingly, I am loved by you.

Lord of the morning
Help me to stop rushing.
I can't love my family in a hurry.
Help me to take time off
To love...

Frank Topping

Holidays

Music

*'By the Sleepy Lagoon' by Eric Coates, played by the London
Symphony Orchestra (from* Music for Pleasure: EMI CFP 40279)

Reading

'Holiday Memory' by Dylan Thomas

There was no need, that holiday morning for the sluggardly boys to
be shouted down to breakfast. Quickly at the bathroom basin they
catlicked their hands and faces, and took the stairs three at a time,
But for all their scramble and scamper, their sisters were always there
before them. Up with the lady lark, they had prinked and frizzed. In
their blossoming dresses, ribboned for the sun, they helped in the
higgledy kitchen.

This was the morning when the sun declared war on the butter,
and the butter ran; when listening at open doors of houses in the
street you might have heard: 'Got your spade?' 'I know I put the
pepper somewhere...' 'Oh, come on, come on...'

And the trams that hissed like ganders took us to the beach, where
all day that August Monday in those radiant, rainless and sky-blue
summers departed, we capered or squealed by the glazed or bashing
sea.

There was cricket on the sand and sand in the sponge cake. Little
naked navvies dug canals. Mothers, gasping under discarded
dresses of daughters who shrilly braved the goblin waves, loudly
warned their proud pink sons to put that jelly-fish down. Fathers,
in the once-a-year sun, took fifty winks. Liquorice allsorts, and
Welsh hearts, were melting. And in the distance, surrounded by disappointed theoreticians, a cross man on an orange box shouted that
holidays were wrong.

I remember the patient, laborious hobby of burying relatives in the
sand, and the princely pastime of pouring sand, from cupped hands
or buckets, down collars and tops of dresses; the shriek, the shake,
the slap.

I remember the smell of the sea and seaweed, wet flesh, wet hair,
wet bathing-dresses, the smell of vinegar on shelled cockles. I
remember, too, the noise of pummelling Punch, and Judy falling, the
steam organ wheezing its waltzes in the fair on the bald seaside field,
and always the ravenous pleading of the gulls, the donkey-bray and
hawker-cry, the clip of the chair attendant's puncher, the motorboat
coughing in the bay, and the same hymn and washing of the sea that

was heard in the Bible. But over all the beautiful beach I remember most the boys and girls playing and tumbling.

As you scooped, in the hob-hot sand, dungeons under a ponderous and cracking castle, your lips said over and over again, 'If only it could be like this for ever and ever amen.'

Prayer

Bless our holidays...
May we return to school refreshed
in mind and body,
May holiday memories be joyful
    and may that spirit remain with us
For ever and ever amen...

Music

Fade up as before, or 'Daytrip to Bangor' by Fiddler's Dram
(Dingle's records DIN 304)

'Ah Just Wanted to Put Things Right'

Music

'The times they are a-changing' sung by Peter, Paul and Mary
(Warner Bros WB 142)

Reading

from The Day of the Sardine *by Sid Chaplin*

Arthur lives with his mother on Tyneside.
He has recently left school and just
finished his first week at a new job.
It is Friday and after being out for
the evening with a gang he has returned
home late.

I walked into a regular little scene of domestic bliss... The Old Lady was sat at one side and Harry at the other, the radio playing softly, and you knew that they'd been having the kind of natter that is possible only between good friends. It caught me on the raw.

'So you're in,' said the Old Lady, switching rapidly from one tone to another. This is a talent I've noticed among the ladies.

'Hello, all,' I said and sat down in my place, which was set.

'His Lordship wants servin'.'

'Aw, Ma, let's have a meal in peace.'

'Look under your plate for your supper.'

'Ah think Ah'll turn in now,' said Harry.

'Stop in and see the entertainment,' said the Old Lady.

'Yes, stay,' I said. 'Join in the fun – when we know what it's all about.' But at the same time I knew what it was all about and also what lay under my plate.

'No thanks, Peg,' he said. 'Ah'll keep me nose out... Ah'm off.'

'Pity he didn't stay to hear ye sayin' your lines,' I remarked to his back.

'Now will ye shut your trap or ye'll have the teapot over your head again,' said the Old Lady. 'Ye talk about me goin' on – ye don't give anybody a chance to keep their tempers and say a word in calmness.' Which, of course, was perfectly true. What is it that keeps you talking when you know it's no good? Especially to older folk. I've noticed they're slower to react – with words. They've the experience but the kids have the wit. But on you go, stirring up trouble...

'Anyway,' I remarked. 'What's all the bawling about – it's a mystery to me, to date.'

'Ah'll give ye credit for more brains than that...'

'Thanks,' I said.

'Ye know what it's about – your pay.'

'What's the matter – can't ye wait?'

'Ah told you that ye'd be on pocket money...then you deliberately go and break into your packet. What's the idea?'

'Let me ask you a question: how d'ye know Ah've broken into it?'

'Well, look under your plate.' But I didn't: I wouldn't give her that pleasure. 'Look under your plate!'

'Ah don't need to look under me plate to know ye've been pokin' about in me room and rakin' about me private property.'

'And Ah don't think much about you,' she said. 'When Ah first started work Ah was proud to go home and hand me pay packet over to your grandma: proud.'

'Times have changed since then...'

'For the worse. Ah'd burn with shame if Ah were you – after the way Ah've toiled and moiled to bring ye up – and on me own – ye turn round and do this.'

'Listen, Ma,' I said, trying to get things onto a reasonable plane. 'Just listen. *Ah'm* going out to work, not you. What was good enough for you doesn't hold for me...oh, it's all right, Ah'll pay me way; Ah'll give you board and lodgings. But Ah'll handle me own money. Ah'll buy me own clothes. Ah'm sick and tired of being taken and told what to wear.'

'You'll hand your pay over – intact.'

'Ah'll pay you board and lodgings – that way we'll both be independent.'

'So's you can splash your money on your fancy monkey suits and keep up wi' your low friends, that's your idea. Well, Ah'm tellin' ye now: Ah'm not havin' it.'

Brushing the plate aside I took up the pay packet and extracted three pound notes: 'There you are. There's your money and be content.' I held them out but didn't get any reaction. So I slapped them bang in the middle of the table.

'All right – Ah'll leave it there an' you can pick it up when Ah've gone in your usual manner.'

'Ah'd burn before Ah'd touch it.'

'Pity you aren't so particular about other things.'

We were both on our feet now and ready to cut. 'What d'ye mean by that crack?'

'That fancy man of yours.'

'Why you little b...'. It wasn't the teapot this time, but the breadboard. Well boy, I'm telling you, I didn't stand to attention. She was berserk, running wild, and coming for me. I ducked and came up and because I was frightened slapped her. She stopped dead. Then she turned and walked over to the chair in the corner and sat down.

'Ah'm sorry, Ma,' I said, following her.

She didn't say a word. She could have said: 'You struck me!' but didn't and I'm bound to admit I admire her for that touch. But I reckon I'd really hurt her. That slap had hit her right on the other solar plexus. 'Ah didn't mean it, Ma, it was just that you were comin' for me. But Ah didn't mean to hit you...like that.' By this time I was kneeling in front of her and she caught hold of my head and drew me to her. I reckon I was bubbling like a bairn.

'Ah'm sorry, Ma. Take the pay, all that's left. Ah shouldn't have done it.' Well, that's what I said, but I'm bound to admit that at the same time I was thinking myself a mug for giving in so easily. And then I was ashamed.

'No, lad,' she said. 'Ah don't want your money. God knows Ah don't want it. Ah just want to put things right between us, and Ah can't, and it gets me mad. Keep the money but be all right with me.'

Prayer

A silent prayer.

Communication (or lack of it)

Music

'Dad's Army' from Norrie Paramor and the Midland Radio Orchestra
BBC Top Tunes (BBC Cassettes REMC 171)

Reading

'The Unexploded Bomb' by C. Day Lewis

Two householders (semi-detached) once found,
Digging in their gardens, a bomb underground –
Half in one's land, half in t'other's with the fence between.
Neighbours they were, but for years had been
Hardly on speaking terms. Now X unbends
To pass a remark across the creosoted fence:
'Look what I've got!... Oh, you've got it too.
Then what, may I ask, are you proposing to do
About this object of yours which menaces my wife,
My kiddies, my property, my whole way of life?'
'Your way of life,' says Y, 'is no credit to humanity.
I don't wish to quarrel; but, since you began it, I
Find your wife stuck-up, your children repel me,
And let me remind you that we too have a telly.
This bomb of mine...'
                                    'I don't like your tone!
And I must point out that, since I own
More bomb than you, to create any tension
Between us won't pay you.'
                                    'What a strange misapprehension!'
Says the other: 'my portion of bomb is near
Six inches longer than yours. So there!'

'They seem,' the bomb muttered in its clenched and narrow
Sleep, 'to take me for a vegetable marrow.'

'It would give me,' said X, 'the greatest pleasure
To come across the fence now with my tape-measure – '
'Oh no,' Y, answered, 'I'm not having you
Trampling my flowerbeds and peering through
My windows.'
                                    'Oho,' snarled X, 'if that's
Your attitude, I warn you to keep your brats
In future from trespassing upon my land,

Or they'll bitterly regret it'.
                    'You misunderstand.
My family has no desire to step on
Your soil; and my bomb is a peace-lover's weapon.'

Called a passing angel, 'If you two shout
And fly into tantrums and keep dancing about,
The thing will go off. It is surely permissible
To say that your bomb, though highly fissible,
Is in another sense one and indivisible;
By which I mean – if you'll forgive the phrase,
Gentlemen – the bloody thing works both ways.
So let me put forward a dispassionate proposal:
Both of you, ring for a bomb-disposal
Unit, and ask them to remove post-haste
The cause of your dispute.'

                    X and Y stared aghast
At the angel. 'Remove my bomb?' they sang
In unison both: 'allow a gang
To invade my garden and pull up the fence
Upon which my whole way of life depends?
Only a sentimental idealist
Could moot it. I, thank God, am a realist.'

The angel fled. The bomb turned over
In its sleep and mumbled, 'I shall soon discover,
If X and Y are too daft to unfuse me,
How the Devil intends to use me.'

Prayer

Lord
Forgive me
That I choose not to hear
The voices that disturb me.
Remind me, again and again,
That you are always listening.

Frank Topping

A Beginning (and an ending)

Music

'Winter' from The Four Seasons by Vivaldi, played by James Galway (RCA Red Seal RL 25034)

Reading

'Georgie and Grandpa' by Lynn Bottomley

Two of the most interesting characters I have met are my little brother Georgie, aged two months and my great Grandfather aged ninety-seven years and two months.

I am interested in both. To my amazement their needs are similar and yet I would have thought that Grandpa would have had fewer needs than Georgie. After all Georgie has need to develop the habits of taking care of himself whereas Grandpa has already learned these things, yet I have heard Mummy say that Georgie is too young to eat meat and Grandpa is now too old for it.

Georgie must be treated with care and gentleness because his bones are weak through lack of age – Grandpa's bones are weak because of over-age.

The house must be quiet when Georgie sleeps because he wakens so easily. Grandpa always goes to bed early and otherwise spends much of his time dozing in his rocking chair.

Grandpa has outgrown the use of a comb and Georgie has not yet grown old enough to need one.

Georgie has not yet the need of a toothbrush. Grandpa stopped cleaning his last remaining tooth four years ago and cannot manage with the new fangled false ones.

Georgie is quite inactive having not yet the strength or ability to walk by himself. Similarly, Grandpa is unable to walk because he has 'screws'!

Little Georgie is without understanding and wisdom, and my Grandfather is past the age of having to understand – his attitude to be wise (as he was a few years ago) is now gone with his memory.

Sounds mean nothing to either of them. Grandfather cannot hear them and Georgie is not yet interested in where they come from or what they mean.

Sometimes Grandpa utters little mumbling noises to himself which mean nothing to either himself or anybody else – unless little Georgie understands them because he also does the some thing – perhaps they are talking to each other in a language of their own!

Both need warmth and are well wrapped up in shawls. Grandpa sucks his pipe while little Georgie sucks his thumb.

Perhaps this is what adults mean when they say, 'He is a chip off the old block!' – Oh, I forgot to tell you that Grandpa's name is George!

Prayer

Help us to be interested in *all* people
and may we *care* for both young and old.

Children's Charter

Music

'She's Leaving Home' by The Beatles (from Sergeant Pepper's Lonely Hearts Club Band: *EMI Columbia TC PCS 7027*)

Reading

'To Parents from their Children' by E. Mildred Nevill

Think about these things.

1 Don't spoil me, I know quite well that I ought not to have all I ask for. I'm only testing you.
2 Don't be afraid to be firm with me. I prefer it. It makes me feel more secure.
3 Don't let me form bad habits. I have to rely on you to detect them in the early stages.
4 Don't make me feel smaller than I am. It only makes me behave stupidly 'big'.
5 Don't correct me in front of people if you can help it. I'll take much more notice if you talk quietly with me in private.
6 Don't make me feel that my mistakes are sins. It upsets my set of values.
7 Don't be too upset when I say 'I hate you'. It isn't you I hate but your power to thwart me.
8 Don't protect me from consequences. I need to learn the painful way sometimes.
9 Don't take too much notice of my small ailments. I am quite capable of trading on them.
10 Don't nag. If you do I shall have to protect myself by appearing deaf.
11 Don't make rash promises. Remember that I feel badly let down when promises are broken.
12 Don't forget that I cannot explain myself as well as I should like. That is why I am not always very accurate.
13 Don't tax my honesty too much. I am easily frightened into telling lies.
14 Don't be inconsistent. That confuses me and makes me lose faith in you.
15 Don't put me off when I ask questions. If you do you will find that I stop asking and seek my information elsewhere.

I wonder if you can see anything of yourself in these points? Sometimes, being a parent is very hard, just as it is very hard for them to understand you and your ups and downs. *The important thing, I think, is that we should try to understand each other's feelings and take the time to listen to each other. Try it.*

Prayer

We need to know ourselves so that we can be true
to ourselves. Help us even when we forget You.

A Mother's Love

Music

'She's Leaving Home' by The Beatles (from Sergeant Pepper's Lonely Hearts Club Band: EMI Columbia TC PCS 7027)

Reading

'From a Mother to her Child' by Erma Bombeck

You may remember the Children's Charter I read to you a little while ago. It consisted of ideas written by a child for a parent to consider. I also asked you to try and understand the other persons point of view as well as your own. Today, I would like you to hear that other point of view:

'You don't love me!' How many times have your children tried that one on you? And how many times have you, as a parent, resisted the urge to tell them how much?

Some day, when my childen are old enough to understand the logic that motivates a mother, I'll tell them.

I loved you enough to irritate you by asking where you were going, with whom, and what time you would get home.

I loved you enough to be silent and let you discover your hand-picked friend was a creep.

I loved you enough to make you return a bar of chocolate with a bite out of it to the shop and confess, 'I stole this.'

I loved you enough to stand over you for two hours while you cleaned your bedroom, a job that would have taken me 15 minutes.

I loved you enough not to make excuses for your lack of respect or your bad manners.

I loved you enough to ignore 'what every other mother' did.

I loved you enough to realize that you would lie about a party being chaperoned but forgive you for it...after discovering I was right.

I loved you enough to let you stumble, fall and fail so that you could learn to stand alone.

I loved you enough to accept you for what you are, not what I wanted you to be.

But most of all, I loved you enough to say no when you hated me for it. That was the hardest part of all.

It is not always easy to understand the other person's point of view. We need a lot of help and time to be able to do so. Even then, some of us cannot manage it because maybe our feelings have been hurt or our pride has been jolted.

Prayer

Help us not to fool ourselves with words, God, with talk of being sorry when we are not sorry, with talk of action when we are too lazy to act. Where our vision is dim, help us to see. Where our hearts are imprisoned by fears, release them. When we see and feel your truth, give us the courage to act.

Avery Brooke

Foolish Dares

Music

Star Wars Main Theme played by Isao Tomita
(from Kosmos: RCA RK 42652)

Reading

'When it's Brave to be Chicken' by Molly Cheston

This story is based on a true event, though some details have been added.

It was the last day of the school holidays. Brian peered out at the moist, misty morning. 'Tomorrow it's sure to be fine and sunny,' he thought. 'It always is the first day back at school.' He crossed to the foot of the stairs. 'Mum, I'm going to call for Gary,' he shouted. 'Bye!' The door slammed after him.

Upstairs a window was flung open and his mother leaned out. 'Don't be late for your dinner,' she warned. Brian strolled down the street and at the corner he met his friend.

'This is Stuart,' said Gary, jerking his chin towards a boy who was with him. 'He's my cousin. He's staying with us.'

Together the boys made their way to the common. For a while they amused themselves balancing on the top of an old stone wall, trying to push each other off. When they tired of that, they sat on the wall, feeling gloomy. There was nothing to do, and the thought of school the next day didn't help.

Brian stared across the countryside. On the one side were pasture and ploughed fields bordered by neat hedges; on the other, rolling heath with rough grass, bracken, clumps of brambles and a line of electricity pylons stretching from skyline to skyline. He knew every inch of it. There was nothing left to explore. 'This place is a dump,' he muttered. 'There's never anything to do.'

'It's better where I come from...' Stuart started.

'Oh, yes, you've got everything at your place, haven't you?' Gary was fed up with his cousin.

'Not everything,' Stuart protested. 'But when there's nothing else to do you can always go climbing. There's one place where they do rock climbing, you know, like you see on the telly. I went climbing once...'

'Bet I could climb higher than you,' muttered Brian.

'It's not as easy as you think,' Stuart said quickly.

'Garn!' Brian laughed scornfully. The next moment the boys were arguing hotly, each sure that *he* was the best climber.

'Prove it!' Brian yelled at Stuart. 'Go on, if you're so good, you show us!'

'How can I?' Stuart was surly. 'You haven't got any rocks or decent trees or anything to climb.'

'We've got that!' Brian pointed to the nearest of the long line of steel pylons which marched like ungainly giants, elbows stiffly out, white insulators hanging where hands should be.

Gary stared. 'The electricity pylons! You're nuts! Those wires are dangerous.'

'You don't have to touch the wires. Go on. You're so clever Stuart. You climb up that pylon, over the top and down the other side. I dare you!'

'I wouldn't be so daft!' Stuart stared at the pylon. 'It's got a Danger notice on it.'

'You're chicken!' Brian sneered.

Gary flared up in defence of his cousin. 'I bet *you* wouldn't do it anyway!'

'Yes I would!' Brian snapped.

'Go on then. I dare you!'

Brian's eyes glittered. 'I'll do it if you will. I dare you to follow me.'

'No!' Stuart protested. 'Don't be daft, Gary.'

'Chicken! Chicken!' taunted Brian. He turned, ran to the nearest pylon and started to climb. A few feet from the ground he turned round, grinning, sure the others would be walking away. But he found Gary right behind him and Stuart was behind Gary. He turned back and pulled himself up to the barbed wire which was stretched across to prevent people climbing any higher. It wasn't easy to get past the wire but he managed it – and still Gary was behind him.

Brian set his teeth and climbed upwards, past the red 'Danger' notice. Surely Gary wouldn't really follow, not all the way? The moment Gary and Stuart stopped, he could stop too. But he couldn't be the first to give up. His pride wouldn't let him.

Below him, Gary looked upwards. He knew they were being stupid. If only Brian would stop.

But Brian didn't stop. He went on towards the first of the cross-bars. There were three of them, six feet apart, holding white insulators from which the heavy wires drooped, before rising, in a slow curve, to the next pylon. The boys knew it was death to touch those wires, but they trusted in their ability to climb over without touching them. What they did *not* know was that there were 33,000 volts of electricity passing through those wires and, when the voltage is as high as that, you don't have to touch the wire – the electricity comes to you. In fact, it can jump quite a large gap.

That is what happened to Brian. One moment he was climbing, the next moment there was a sheet of flame as the electricity passed through his body and down to the ground. Brian was killed instantly. Gary was so badly shocked and burnt that he fell to the ground and was killed. Stuart was burned too and fell, but he did not have so far to fall and he survived.

When he was interviewed in hospital, Stuart was asked why he had been so stupid as to climb the pylon. He said: 'I didn't want them to think I was chicken.'

Prayer

Help us to find the courage to 'be chicken'.
Sometimes it takes real courage to be the
first to give up. Let us think beyond the
moment ruled by our stubborn pride and remember
that our actions not only involve ourselves.
Help us to think of those who love us.

'You're Going Home, Not Knowing?'

Music

'Tie a Yellow Ribbon' sung by Tony Orlando and Dawn (Pikwick SSP 307)

Reading

'Hearts of Oak' by Pete Hamill

I first heard this story from a girl who said she had been one of the participants. In the years since, I've heard of several other versions. Probably it is one of those strange bits of folklore that emerge every few years. The characters change, the message endures. I like to think that it did happen, somewhere, sometime...

They were going to Florida – three boys and three girls. When they boarded the bus, they were clutching sandwiches and wine, dreaming of golden beaches and sea-tides as the grey cold of New York vanished behind them.

As the bus rumbled south, they began to notice Vingo. He sat in front of them, dressed in a plain, ill-fitting suit, never moving, his dusty face masking his age. He chewed the inside of his lip a lot, frozen into some personal cocoon of silence.

Deep into the night, outside Washington, the bus pulled in at a roadside restaurant, and everybody got off except Vingo. He sat rooted to his seat, and the young people began to wonder about him, trying to imagine his life: perhaps he was a sea captain, a runaway from his wife, an old soldier going home. When they went back to the bus, one of the girls sat beside him and introduced herself.

'We're going to Florida,' she said brightly. 'I hear it's beautiful.'

'It is,' he said quietly, as if remembering something he had tried to forget.

'Want some wine?' she asked. He smiled and took a swig. He thanked her and retreated again into his silence. After a while, she went back to the others, and Vingo slept.

In the morning, they awoke outside another restaurant, and this time Vingo went in. The girl insisted that he join them. He seemed very shy, and ordered black coffee and smoked nervously as the young people chattered. When they returned to the bus, the girl sat with Vingo again, and after a while, slowly and painfully, he told his story. He had been in jail in New York for the past four years, and now he was going home.

'Are you married?'

'I don't know.'

'You don't know?' she said.

'Well, while I was inside I wrote to my wife,' he said. 'I told her that I was going to be away a long time, and that if she couldn't stand it, if the kids kept asking questions, if it hurt too much, well, she could forget me. I'd understand. Get somebody new, I said – she's a wonderful woman, really something – and forget about me. I told her she didn't have to write. She didn't. Not for three and a half years.'

'And you're going home now, not *knowing*?'

'Yes,' he said shyly. 'Well, last week, when I was sure the parole was coming through, I wrote to her again. We used to live in Brunswick, and there's a big oak tree just as you come into town. I told her that if she'd take me back, she should put a yellow hand-kerchief on the tree, and I'd get off and come home. If she didn't want me, forget it – no handkerchief, and I'd go on through.'

The girl told the others, and soon all of them were in it, caught up in the approach of Brunswick, looking at the pictures Vingo showed them of his wife and three children – the woman handsome in a plain way, the children still unformed in the cracked, much handled snapshots.

Now they were twenty miles from Brunswick, and the young people all sat at window seats, waiting for the approach of the great oak tree. The bus acquired a dark, hushed mood, full of the silence of absence and lost years. Vingo stopped looking, tightening his face into the ex-con's mask, as if fortifying himself against another disappointment.

Then Brunswick was ten miles away, and then five. Suddenly, all the young people were out of their seats, screaming and shouting and crying, doing small dances of exultation. All except Vingo.

Vingo sat there stunned, looking at the oak tree. It was covered with yellow handkerchiefs – twenty of them, thirty of them, maybe hundreds, a tree that stood like a banner of welcome billowing in the wind. As the young people shouted, the old convict rose from his seat and made his way to the front of the bus to go home.

Prayer

Help us, O God, to do some little
thing today that will make the world
a better place because we have been here.

Finders Keepers

Music

'Cagney and Lacey' (from Telly Hits by Various Artists:
Stylus/BBC BBSC 508)

Reading

from 'The Goalkeeper's Revenge' by Bill Naughton

All of us know the meaning of the phrase, 'Finders keepers', but have we ever asked how true it really is?

I used to be so fond of oranges that I could suck one after the other the whole day long – until the time that the policeman gave me a scare at the dock gates when he caught me almost redhanded with seventeen hidden away in my various pockets, and he locked me up, and ever since then I've never looked at an orange – because that gave me my fill of them.

I was driving a little pony-and-cart for the Swift Delivery Company in those days, and lots of my pick-ups were at the docks, where I could put on a handy sample load and be back at the depot before the other carriers had watered their mares.

Now I was not what you call a proper fiddler, and I did not make a practice of knocking things off just because they didn't belong to me, like some people do, but just the same, it was very rare I came off those docks without a bit of something to have a chew at during the day.

Say they were unloading a banana boat; well, I used to draw my little cart alongside. There were often loose bunches that had dropped off the main stalks. And when the chance came I would either make a quick grab, or some friendly foot would shove them towards me. Then I used to duck them out of sight under my brat. The brat was an open apron made from a Tate and Lyle sugar-bag, supposed to be good protection against rain and rough wear, but mine was used mostly for concealment. And for the rest of that day I'd be munching away at bananas, even though I hadn't a passion for them like I had for oranges...

I got caught because the string of my brat broke, and Pongo (the bobby on duty), after looking over my load, noticed my somewhat bulging pockets. He made me draw the pony-and-cart to one side, and then he took me into his cabin and went through my pockets. There were seventeen oranges in all, and he placed them carefully on the table.

'An example has to be made,' he said, 'of somebody or other – and I reckon you're the unlucky one. Now, my lad, what have you to say for yourself?'

I said nothing. I was dead frightened, but I forced myself to keep my mouth shut. I had read too many detective stories to make the mistake of blabbing. *Anything you say may be used in evidence against you.* I kept that firm in my mind, and I refused to be interrogated. Pongo, who did not care for my attitude, said, 'Righto, I'll go off and bring a colleague as a witness.' And with that he went, carefully locking the door behind him.

I felt awful then. It was the suspense. I looked at the walls, I looked at the door, and I looked at my brat with the broken string. I thought of how I would get sacked and get sentenced...

There was no escape. I was there – and the evidence was there before me on the table – and Pongo had gone for his mate to be a witness. I was ruined for life.

'Oh, my God,' I moaned in anguish, 'whatever shall I do?'

'Eat'em!' spoke a voice in my head.

'Eh?' I asked. 'Eat 'em?'

'Yeh, that's right,' replied this inner voice – 'and then the evidence will be gone. But be quick about it.'

I thought for half a second – then I snatched an orange, peeled it in a jiff, popped it in my mouth, crushed the juice out and swallowed it, swallowing the orange, and I was just about to squirt out the pips when the voice cried:

'No!'

'Eh?'

'You have to swallow them too!'

'Yes – peel an' all! Evidence.'

'Oh-oh, of course,' and I forced the pips to the back of my mouth and took a handful of peel to help get them down my gullet.

'Don't bother to chew,' said the voice, 'it's a race against time.'

It certainly was. After the first orange I took out my penknife and cut the fruit into chunks and gulped them down fast...

It may be oranges or any number of things, but we must remember, 'finding' doesn't necessarily mean 'keeping'.

Prayer

Sometimes we find it very hard to be
honest – temptations come thick and
fast in this busy world.
Help us to be honest and true to ourselves.
Help us also to admit our wrongs and to
accept fair blame.

When Dad Left Home

Music

Air on the G String by Bach, played by Eugene Ormandy
(from Commercial Break: CBS Classics 40-61836)

Reading

'One Saturday' by Vanessa Wager

The morning started off like any other Saturday. Mum was cooking breakfast for dad. She never cooked breakfast for me. I would have a glass of orange or a cup of coffee. After breakfast mum and dad would get ready to go shopping. I hated shopping so I would make some excuse to stay home and watch the television.

Mum and dad took about half an hour to get ready. Mum was the worst of the two. She would start shouting or get in a panic if she could not find something. I was glad to see them drive off in the car. I made sure I had everything I needed beside me when watching the morning film.

Jocky, my dog, would either sleep or go in the garden while I was involved in the film. After the film I would take Jocky for a long walk up the Hill. Up there I was in a different world. There was just Jocky and me. I would then pretend I was somebody else in a different land. When I was near home I would have to come back to reality.

When I walked indoors I felt something bad had happened. Mum was putting the shopping away and at the same time she was crying. I asked several times what was wrong. She didn't seem to hear me. In the end I shouted at her. She turned round quickly and just looked at me. She did not have to say a word; her face said it all. I ran upstairs and went in their room. His clothes had gone and some pictures that used to be on the dressing table. Tears were coming out like a fountain. Jocky jumped on the bed and would not stop licking my face. I just sat there in a daze. Mum got herself together and made us a cup of tea with some cake. She explained what had happened.

It was about two years later that he got in contact with us. I visit him and his new wife when they come to stay in England. I still have nightmares about that day when Dad left home.

Prayer

'God moves in a mysterious way',
Give us strength and patience to understand.

Maybe Tomorrow

Music

'Streets of London' by Ralph McTell (Reprise, K 14380)

Reading

'Dreams of Old Age' by Karen Wallis

Number sixty-six Victoria Street was a replica of many other rambling boarding houses in the East End of London; dilapidated yet proud. Its walls were thick with damp mould and its furniture wriggling and crumbling with woodworm. The carpets reeked with neglect and the windows coated with cobwebs and forever curtained by the trailing ivy. The house and its contents were dying a slow, weary death.

The attic balanced precariously on top of the decrepit bricks. A shower of sunlight forced its way through the dust-laden glass, scattering pin points of brilliance over the once patterned rug. A small electric heater gave a sparse glow of warmth to a deformed hand that stretched feebly out to claim it. Its owner sat hunched in her faithful rocking chair, comforted by the slow relaxing rhythm as it moved backwards then forwards. On her lap lay her most treasured possession, her only link with the past years: her family album. Countless times had she flicked through the musty pages to recall the memories that helped her survive. Now she opened the book once more and her thin lips cracked into a smile and her intriguing blue eyes wrinkled with silent laughter.

Yet where were these people now, those whom she had loved and who, she felt, had loved her? Her husband had been torn from her by the evils of war and her only child Elizabeth, was too proud to be seen with her withering mother. 'Mad Ellen' they called her; loveable but eccentric, not good enough for her daughter, who cared only for climbing the social ladder. Ellen knew she was a burden; someone who must be looked after, but pushed aside, unwanted. Her laughter turned to tears. 'I'm not mad!' and although her mind shrieked it, her voice merely whispered. She hugged her under-nourished frame and peered around her cold hovel. Familiar faces looked and laughed at her. She picked one up and smashed it to the floor. 'Hypocrites!' she hissed vehemently.

She squinted at her clock, a relic like herself. 'Time to be off,' she muttered, wrenching her bones from the chair by the inadequate heat of the fire. She gathered her moth-eaten coat and groped blindly as she made her way down the groaning stairs. Her unstable feet frightened her. One day she would fall and her life would be at an end. This knowledge terrified her; death was so near. However, maybe it would be a happy release; her daughter would think so.

She thrust her resisting body out into the bitter wind shivering violently; she mingled into the indifferent crowds; a rambling old woman, like many others in the city...

'All these people! So many! Too many! Not enough food. Was not like this in my day. Oh no, not in my day...'

Again she was living in the past, scolding her young daughter and reassuring herself of the safe return of her husband from the cruel war. Children laughed and scorned her while adults looked with pity but then dismissed the sorry sight. Ellen had learnt to ignore them. Automatically, she made her way to the shelter of a shop entrance and brought out her ancient mouth organ and played the tunes she had learnt as a child, oblivious to those who scoffed at her and called her a 'scrounger' and a 'fake' yet gently acknowledging those who dropped money into her weather-beaten hat...

'I think I'll take a stroll in the park and then I'll satisfy my appetite at the Ritz!' She laughed a croaking, unusual laugh...

Her daily walk in the park always revived her, clearing her brain of the bitterness that enveloped it... She threw stale bread to the ducks who looked up expectantly for more.

'You're so very ungrateful,' she grumbled.

'Like Elizabeth,' she added.

Finding her favourite seat she made herself comfortable on the wooden bench. She stretched her crooked legs. The weak warmth of the sun was welcoming. Her eyelids relaxed and she slept a while. After an hour her inbuilt alarm awoke her and she started on her long, weary journey home, to her local cafe, and then to bed.

At seven o'clock, finally, she opened the door of her rooftop bed-sit. The cold danced through her, its spiteful fingers clawing her whole body. She wrapped herself in the only insulation she knew: brown paper.

'Like an old parcel no one wants,' she croaked, as she crawled into her bed with its insufficient blankets.

Maybe tomorrow would be different. Maybe tomorrow Elizabeth would come and see her.

Prayer

Let us think for a few moments about
those for whom tomorrow holds little hope.
May our thoughts offer some comfort.

See Me

Music

Canon in D Major by Pachelbel, played by The Munich Pro Arte Chamber Orchestra (RCA Gold Seal GK 25240)

Reading

'Plea by a Retarded Child' by Rita Dranginis

You look at me with pity, concern or indifference,
For I am a retarded child.
But you only see outside me.
If I could express myself,
I would tell you what I am inside.

I am very much like you,
I feel pain and hunger.
I cannot ask politely for a glass of water,
I know the parched, dry feeling of thirst.
I itch when mosquitoes bite me,
And run when l see a bee.
I feel cosy drinking cocoa in the kitchen
When a snowstorm blusters outside.

I had a heaviness inside
When I left my mother to board the mini-bus for school.
My eyes darted back and forth
Seeking escape,
But knowing there was none.
When my sister takes me to the playground
And children call me names,
She cries, and takes me home.
Then I feel warm and dizzy,
And it's hard for me to breathe.
Mother's eyes were wet;
She holds me and tells me a story,
And I forget the children's jeers.
When I dress myself, and mother pats my head
And says,
'Good job, Jim',
I feel...big,
As big as Greg who is in the second form.
I am a child in age now,
And in ability always.

I find the touch of soft toys
And snuggly dogs comforting.
I love the toys of childhood
A kite, a balloon, a wagon to pull.
I like to let go at the top of a slide,
And after dizzy seconds, find myself at the bottom.
I like sledges on soft snow,
The wetness of rain on my forehead.

Though it is comforting to be babied
I am less dependent when people treat me as a big toy.
I don't want their sympathy,
I want their respect for what I can do.
I am slow, and many things you take for granted
Are hard for me.
I can hardly understand what tomorrow means.
It took me months to learn to pedal the tall blue tricycle,
But I was so proud when at last
Both feet pedalled in the same direction
And the wheels went forward.
How happy I was
When I turned the right tap to get a drink of water.
I didn't want to ever turn it off.

If I can learn at my own pace,
And still be accepted,
I can fit into a world where slowness is suspect.
Think of me first as a person who hurts
And loves
And feels joy.
And know I am a child to encourage
And direct
And smile
And say hallo.

Even that is enough.

Prayer

Help us to look beyond the first impressions.
Too often we dismiss what we do not fully understand.
Give us patience and understanding.

The Most Gentle Person

Music

Canon in D Major by Pachelbel, played by The Munich Pro Arte Chamber Orchestra (RCA Gold Seal GK 25240)

Reading

from Unforgettable Christy Brown *by Stephen Rudley and C L Lynes*

Christy Brown was born in Ireland in 1932. He had been born a 'blue, asphyxiated infant'. By the time doctors regulated his breathing, the part of the brain that controls muscular co-ordination had been damaged. His arms twisted and flailed. He could not sit without support or crawl. He dribbled constantly.

At that time very little was known about Christy's condition – cerebral palsy. Doctors diagnosed him as mentally defective. Nothing could be done, they said. Put him in an institution.

The Browns refused. They would care for their child at home with his brothers and sisters, at Stannaway Road in Kimmage, a working-class suburb of Dublin. Mrs Brown was convinced that her son was not an imbecile, and set out to prove it.

Day after day, year after year, she read to Christy, talked to him, touched him, trying to get him to respond. And her husband, despite long hours as a bricklayer, washed him, helped him in the lavatory, dressed him. But Christy did not improve.

For Christy, those first years were like a strange dream. He could hear and see, feel and think, but had no way to tell anyone. He could not even nod his head. He longed to let his family know he was there. How could he break through?

Then one day when he was five, Christy sat propped up with pillows on the kitchen floor watching his sister Mona write on a slate. Suddenly his left foot shot out, grasped the chalk between its toes and scribbled wildly across the slate. He had never used his foot before.

In his own words, 'I tried again. I put out my foot and made a wild jerking stab with the chalk which produced a very crooked line and nothing more. Mother held the slate steady for me.'

'Try again, Chris,' she whispered in my ear.

'Again.' I did. I stiffened my body and put my left foot out again for the third time. I drew one side of the letter. I drew half the other side. Then the stick of chalk broke and I was left with a stump. I wanted to fling it away and give up. Then I felt my mother's hand on my shoulder. I tried once more. Out went my foot. I shook, I sweated and strained every muscle. My hands were so tightly clenched that my finger-nails bit into the flesh. I set my teeth so hard that I nearly pierced my lower lip. Everything in the room swam until the faces around me were mere patches of white. But – I drew it – *the letter A.* I looked up. I saw my mother's face for a moment, tears on her cheeks. Then my father stopped and hoisted me on to his shoulder.

I had done it! It had started – the thing that was to give my mind its chance of expressing itself. True, I couldn't speak with my lips. But now I would speak through something more lasting than spoken words – written words.

That one letter scrawled on the floor with a broken bit of yellow chalk gripped between my toes, was my road to a new world, my key to mental freedom. It was to provide a source of relaxation to the tense, taut thing that was I, which panted for expression behind twisted mouth.'

From this beginning, Christy learned to read, and paint. When he was 22 years old his autobiography *My Left Foot* was published. From the proceeds he bought an electric typewriter and he was then able to keep pace with his thoughts. Christy continued to create, painting constantly and producing a wealth of stories, poems and articles. In 1970 he produced his novel *Down All The Days* and suddenly, Christy was a celebrity. Critics called him a genius.

One evening at a party, Christy saw a lovely blonde woman talking to friends. She turned and smiled at him. Christy looked away. He felt embarrassed, painfully self-conscious as he sat in his wheelchair. Then, all of a sudden, she was sitting beside him, talking. Her name was Mary Carr and she was a dental nurse. On October 6th 1972 they were married. Christy signed the marriage register with his left foot.

The announcement in the New York Times quoted Mary as saying, 'He is the most gentle person I have ever known and I love him very much.' Mary became Christy's anchor, his companion and his best critic. He called her 'the major miracle of my life.'

Christy Brown died on September 6th 1981, aged 49. He and Mary had been married for nine years.

Prayer

Teach us to care for each other and to
have the courage to show our compassion,
even when others may not have the strength
to do so.

Fool's Paradise

Music

Overture from Fiddler on the Roof *by Jerry Bock and performed by the original London cast (CBS 31519)*

Reading

from Zlateh the Goat and Other Stories *by Isaac Bashevis Singer.*

Somewhere, sometime, there lived a rich man whose name was Kadish. He had an only son who was called Atzel. In the household of Kadish there lived a distant relative, an orphan girl, called Aksah. Both Atzel and Aksah were about the same age and it was taken for granted that when they grew up they would be married.

But when they had grown up, Atzel suddenly became ill. It was a sickness no one had ever heard of before: Atzel imagined that he was dead.

How did such an idea come to him? An old nurse had told him once that in paradise it was not necessary to work or to study. In paradise one ate the meat of wild oxen and the flesh of whales; one drank the wine that the Lord reserved for the just; one slept late; one had no duties.

Atzel was lazy by nature and since the only way to get to paradise was to die, he had made up his mind to do just that as quickly as possible. He thought about it so much that soon he began to imagine that he *was* dead.

Many doctors were called in to examine Atzel, but before long Atzel began to eat less, and he rarely spoke. His family feared that he would die.

In despair, Kadish went to consult a great specialist, celebrated for his knowledge and wisdom. His name was Dr Yoetz. After listening to a description of Atzel's illness, he said to Kadish, 'I promise to cure your son in eight days, on one condition. You must do whatever I tell you to, no matter how strange it may seem.'

When Dr Yoetz arrived, he was taken to Atzel's room. The boy lay on his bed, pale and thin from fasting.

The doctor took one look at Atzel and called out, 'Why do you keep a dead body in the house? Why don't you make a funeral?

Although Kadish and his wife were bewildered by the doctor's words, they remembered Kadish's promise, and went immediately to make arrangements for the funeral.

The doctor requested that a room be prepared to look like paradise. The walls were hung with white satin. The windows were shuttered, and curtains tightly drawn. Candles burned day and night. The servants, dressed in white with wings on their backs, were to play angels.

Atzel was placed in an open coffin, and a funeral ceremony was held. Atzel was so exhausted with happiness that he slept right through it. When he awoke, he found himself in a room he didn't recognise. 'Where am I?' he asked.

'In paradise, my lord,' a winged servant replied.

'I'm terribly hungry,' Atzel said. 'I'd like some whale flesh and sacred wine.'

Atzel ate ravenously. When he had finished, he declared he wanted to rest. Two angels undressed him, and carried him to a bed with silken sheets and purple velvet canopy. Atzel immediately fell into a deep and happy sleep.

When he awoke, it was morning but it could just as well have been night. The shutters were closed, and the candles were burning. As soon as the servants saw that Atzel was awake, they brought in exactly the same meal as the day before.

Atzel asked, 'Don't you have any milk, coffee, fresh rolls and butter?'

'No, my lord. In paradise one always eats the same food,' the servant replied.

'Is it already day, or is it still night?' Atzel asked.

'In paradise there is neither day nor night.'

Atzel again ate the fish, meat, fruit, and drank the wine, but his appetite was not as good as it had been. When he had finished, he asked, 'What is the time?'

'In paradise time does not exist,' the servant answered.

'What shall I do now?' Atzel questioned.

'In paradise, my lord, one doesn't do anything.'

'Where are the other saints?' Atzel enquired.

'In paradise each family has a place of its own.'

'Can't one go visiting?'

'In paradise the dwellings are too far from each other for visiting. It would take thousands of years to go from one to the other.'

'When will my family come?' Atzel asked.

'Your father still has 20 years to live, your mother 30. And as long as they live they can't come here.'

'What about Aksah?'

'She has 50 years to live.'

'Do I have to be alone all that time?'

'Yes, my lord.'

For a while Atzel shook his head, pondering. Then he asked, 'What is Aksah going to do?'

'Right now she's mourning for you. But sooner or later she will forget you, meet another young man, and marry. That's how it is with the living.'

Atzel got up and began to walk to and fro. For the first time in years he had a desire to do something, but there was nothing to do in his paradise. He missed his father; he longed for his mother; he yearned for Aksah. He wished he had something to study; he wanted to ride his horse, to talk to friends.

The time came when he could no longer conceal his sadness. He remarked to. one of the servants, 'I see now that it is not as bad to live as I had thought.'

'To live, my lord, is difficult. One has to study, to work, do business. Here everything is easy.'

'I would rather chop wood and carry stones than sit here. And how long will this last?'

'Forever.'

'Stay here forever?' Atzel began to tear his hair in grief. 'I'd rather kill myself.'

'A dead man can't kill himself.'

On the eighth day, when Atzel had reached the deepest despair, one of the servants, as had been arranged, came to him and said, 'My lord, there has been a mistake. You are not dead. You must leave paradise.'

'I'm alive?'

'Yes, you are alive, and I will bring you back to earth.'

Atzel was beside himself with joy. The servant blindfolded him, and after leading him back and forth through the long corridors of the house, brought him to the room where his family was waiting and uncovered his eyes.

It was a bright day, and the sun shone through the open windows. In the garden outside, the birds were singing and the bees buzzing. Joyfully, he embraced and kissed his parents and Aksah.

And to Aksah he said, 'Do you still love me?'

'Yes I do, Atzel. I could not forget you.'

'If that is so, it is time we got married.'

It was not long before the wedding took place.

Atzel and Aksah were extremely happy, and both lived to a ripe old age. Atzel stopped being lazy and became the most diligent merchant in the whole region.

It was not until after the wedding that Atzel learned how Dr Yoetz had cured him, and that he had lived in a fool's paradise.

Prayer

Let us think for a moment about our own lives.
We do not always consider fairly the ordinary
things around us which help to enrich our
days. Teach us to enjoy our lives to the full.

You're a Walking Marvel

Music

'Match of the Day' (from Sporting Themes by Various Artists: BBC Cassette no. ZCR 348)

Reading

'Incredible Human Body' by Harvey Kirk

Did you know your ears are still growing, even though the other parts of your body have stopped? And that if you lived to be 1,000, your ears would be as large as an elephant's?

The quality of your hearing varies according to the time of day. It is at its worst at lunchtime and at its keenest during the early morning.

You may not have a hairy chest, but your whole body is covered with hairs – more than 500,000. The only hairless areas are the palms of your hands and the soles of your feet. And you may not think the hair on your head is very strong, but it is as strong as aluminium. A narrow stretch of rope woven from human hair has supported the weight of a small car.

Your skull is as strong as steel, though proportionately it weighs only a fifth as much.

You think you've got nice big blue eyes? Not so. Blue eyes are really red and only appear to be blue. The iris, the coloured part of the eye, is covered with tiny blood vessels which, seen through the cornea at the front of the eye, look blue (in the same way veins look blue when seen through the skin.)

The fact that you blink several hundred times a day means you spend a considerable amount of your waking life unable to see a thing.

The hardest part of your body is the enamel on your teeth – it is even harder than ivory.

Your hands are probably your most complex instruments, capable of performing thousands of jobs with precision. Just to grasp something brings into play a host of muscles, joints and tendons – from the shoulders to the finger-tips. Taking a spoonful of soup, for instance, involves more than 30 joints and 50 muscles.

Few people have absolutely healthy feet and you are probably no exception. During an average day, your feet take a sledge-hammer pounding equivalent to more than a thousand tons. They can support the weight of a 14-stone man on a base less than one third of a square foot in area without fatigue. This is achieved by an astonishing arrangement of bones and joints – for a quarter of all the bones in your body are in your feet.

The human heart beats about 100,000 times a day and about 40,000,000 times a year. Normally it beats 70 to the minute, but it often changes its rate to keep pace with music or the rapid beat of drums. It can be made to pulse to almost any rhythm and automatically picks up the beat set for it.

You may not have noticed it, but you are a little lop-sided. If you could be folded in half longways, your halves would not match perfectly. Usually the left leg is a shade shorter than the right. One arm is longer, one ear bigger and there is likely to be more hair on one side of the head than the other.

Your body contains four ounces of sugar, enough chlorine to disinfect two swimming pools, 50 quarts of water, three pounds of calcium and 24 pounds of carbon. You have enough phosphorus to make 20,000 match heads, enough fat for 10 bars of soap, enough iron to make a two-inch nail, enough sulphur to rid a dog of fleas and enough glycerine to explode a naval shell.

It all comes gift-wrapped in 20 square feet of skin.

Prayer

Thank you for the wonders of the universe. Help us to respect and care for our bodies and not to abuse or waste the gifts so freely given.

Just Gossip?

Music

'The Windmills of your Mind' (from The Phase 4 World of Thrillers
by Various Artists: Decca CSP 160)

Reading

based on 'Thou shalt not bear false witness'

Bearing false witness doesn't just mean giving false evidence against
someone in a law court. It means all this business of tittle-tattle,
passing on damaging tales about people, enjoying a bit of scandal,
tearing someone else's reputation to shreds. Once that sort of talk
starts you never know where it is going to end up.

There was once a simple old French peasant-woman who was
rather given to this sort of malicious gossip about other people. She
was always spreading scandals. One day, after she had caused a lot
of trouble, the village priest – a man everyone loved and trusted –
tackled her and tried to make her see what she was really doing. But
she couldn't see any harm in a bit of talk she said – after all, *words*
couldn't hurt anybody. So the priest said, 'Well, it's a bad business.
Just the same, God can't forgive you until you do realise how wrong
it is.' Then he said, 'I'll tell you what. Will you do something for me?
Will you take this sack full of feathers?' (he gave her a small sack
with thousands of tiny feathers in it) 'and just walk down the lane to
the windmill and back, and scatter these feathers in the wind?'

'Yes, if you like,' said the old woman, thinking it was a pretty silly
thing to ask anybody to do. It wasn't far to the windmill. So, off she
went, scattering the feathers far and wide, in handfuls. She was back
in five minutes.

'Now,' said the priest, 'will you do something else for me? Will
you take the sack and go and collect them all up again?'

Off went the old woman, thinking this was even more silly; but
she soon found out it was a bigger job than she had thought. Some of
the feathers had blown into the hedges and she spent a long time
picking them out one by one, and scratching her fingers on the
thorns. Others had blown off across the meadows and had got lost in
the grass. Hundreds of them had blown so far in the wind that she
could never hope to find them at all. At last, after about three hours
of hard work, she came back with only a miserable handful of feathers
at the bottom of the sack.

'So, there you are,' said the priest. 'That's what happens to your
idle and malicious words. You scatter them around and they travel

far and wide and do far more harm than you can ever imagine – and you can *never* get them back again.'

And the old woman understood.

Prayer

Today, if I hear something
About a friend or colleague,
Prevent me from making a judgement that is unkind.
If I read in the paper
About the mistakes of a fellow man or woman,
Do not let my mind turn to gossip.
Help me to see the best in people.
And when I hear opinions,
May I remember that they are *only* opinions,
For only you know the truth.

Frank Topping

A Smile

Music

*'The Easy Winners' by Scott Joplin, played by Ronnie Price
(from The Scott Joplin Ragtime Album: Embassy 40-31043)*

Reading

'Value of a Smile' (Anon)

A smile costs nothing, but gives much. It enriches those who receive, without making poorer those who give it. It takes but a moment, but the memory of it sometimes lasts forever. No one is so rich and mighty that he can get along without it and no one is so poor but that he can be made rich by it.

A smile creates happiness in the home, fosters good will in business and is the countersign of friendship. It brings rest to the weary, cheer to the discouraged, sunshine to the sad and it is Nature's best anti-dote for trouble. Yet, it cannot be bought, begged, borrowed or stolen, for it is something that is of no value to anyone until it is given away.

Some people are too tired to give you a smile. Give them one of yours, as no one needs a smile so much as he who has no more to give...

> In this morning light
> The faces of my family
> Smile at me from a photograph
> And I find myself smiling back.
> A fleeting moment of happiness
> Trapped on a film
> Bringing me happiness now.
> At this moment I can hear them
> Moving about the house,
> Preparing for another day.
> Today there will be difficulties and problems,
> Maybe we will argue, as people do.
> But today Lord
> Let there be moments of happiness.
>
> In this morning light
> I remember an act of kindness,
> A gesture of love from a small child.
> I remember laughing
> Until the tears ran down our faces;

I remember the excitement,
The shouting, the rocking of the boat
When we landed our first fish.
I remember Christmas trees
And birthday parties,
Sunny days on the beach,
Wet days tramping over hills. *thro' the rain with the shopping & the present*
Lord of the morning,
Help me to remember these moments
With gratitude as I go about
The ordinary things of today.
Lord of the morning
If happiness is sharing,
Loving, giving, understanding,
Help me to share the good things of this day.
Help me to be loving
And thoughtful with family and friends. *and teacher*
Help me to be generous in giving
Time and attention.
Help me to be understanding
When things go wrong
So that this day may be a day of love,
A day to remember.
Lord of the morning, help me...

Frank Topping

A smile costs nothing, but gives much. It enriches those who receive, without making poorer those who give it. It takes but a moment, but the memory of it sometimes lasts for ever.

Prayer

In a few quiet moments, let us think
about the day to come.

Blessing the Bride

Music

Widor Toccata in F played by Francis Jackson at York Minster
(Alpha AVME 016)

Reading

'English Country Customs' by Virginia Black

With the reappearance of new growth and the promise of plenty all round, June was always considered a lucky month for weddings in England. From Saxon times the bridal pair were showered with crumbs of bread to ensure that the couple would never want. In Devon the bride received a gift of nuts which would bring many children. In Nottinghamshire wheat was thrown signifying 'bread for life and pudding forever', and in time the traditional bread has become the Bride Cake. In the North Riding of Yorkshire (now North Yorkshire) races were run round the village to secure the cake and a piece placed under the pillow of an unmarried girl brought dreams of her future husband.

Neither was Bride Cake the only prize. As recently as 1894 the Tudor custom of a race for the bride's garter was still practised in parts of England – a tumultuous affair with no holds barred among young men on fast horses to secure the favour. Successive ages, which abhorred Tudor exuberance, often criticised the unseemliness which these high spirited escapades produced.

Until the nineteenth century it was common for bridal parties to walk to church through floral arches along a route strewn with flowers. A sprig of white myrtle from the bride's posy – the evergreen leaves signifying everlasting love – was planted beside the door of her new home. Nearly all these cuttings struck and almost every cottage had its myrtle bush. Naturally there were many customs concerning all aspects of this important ceremony, beginning with the day of the week to be chosen:

> Monday for wealth, Tuesday for health,
> Wednesday, best day of all,
> Thursday for losses, Friday for crosses,
> Saturday, no luck at all.

Bridal parties often circled the church three times in a sunwise direction for luck before entering and, as it was considered unlucky for the church clock to strike while the wedding was in progress, the party might wait outside until the time was right.

Once married there were still more significant rites to be observed. At Chaddleworth, Berkshire, whoever first climbed the steep step of the church door was 'master' for life so that there was a rush between the bridal pair to be first to accomplish this important feat! It was also important that the bride enter her new home by the front door without stumbling, hence the custom for the groom to carry his bride across the threshold.

To the present day the girl who catches the bride's posy is believed to be the next to marry, and, so that no-one should be left out of the romantic games, all could observe the custom of carefully peeling an apple in one long strip so that the peel could be thrown over the shoulder to fall miraculously into the initial of the husband (or wife) to be.

But such was the magic of Midsummer's Eve that the girl who threw hempseed over her shoulder would 'see' her future husband, perhaps her Valentine of the previous February, for it is on this day, according to ancient belief, that the birds, with heaven's blessing, choose their mates.

Prayer

We ask that you guide and bless
those who are about to join in
marriage.

The Art of Marriage

Music

Widor Toccata in F played by Francis Jackson at York Minster
(Alpha AVME 016)

Reading

'The Art of Marriage' (Anon)

You may remember the old country customs surrounding marriage which I read aloud to you a little while ago. Today I would like to share with you some of the ideals of such a relationship. I wonder what you think about these things?

A good marriage must be created.
In marriage, the little things are the big things.
It is never being too old to hold hands,
It is remembering to say 'I Love You' at least once a day.

It is never going to sleep angry.
It is having a mutual sense of values and common objectives.
It is standing together and facing the world.
It is forming a circle of love that gathers the whole family.

It is speaking words of appreciation and demonstrating gratitude in thoughtful ways.

It is having the capacity to forgive and forget.

It is giving each other an atmosphere in which each can grow.

It is not only marrying the right person
It is being the right partner.

Quite a list, isn't it? And yet, if we look at it closely many of those qualities are the very ones which enable all of us to get along together with our family and friends. Is this how you had ever thought of marriage?

Prayer

Help us to understand that we
are responsible for each other's
happiness. We need you to guide
us towards a caring and considerate
attitude.

'Ere, Where's Me 'Andbag?'

Music

'Doctor Kildare' Theme by Alyn Ainsworth (from TV Music Spectacular: Ampro UK AMP 002)

Reading

from One Pair of Feet *by Monica Dickens*

The writer is a nurse in her first year of training in a war-time hospital. She and Chris, a senior nurse, are on night duty in a women's ward.

They had had several operation cases in the late afternoon and evening, and the last one, an old lady of seventy, had come back from the Theatre only just alive. 'She won't last long,' said Sister, getting up again to feel her barely perceptible pulse. 'I've rung up her people, but I doubt whether they'll get here in time.' Automatically, she straightened the sheet over the dying woman and left us. There was nothing more she could do.

Sister Adams was off that night, and Sister Gilbert came tiptoeing up at ten o'clock with Mrs Colley's relations. The husband was a humble old man with faded blue eyes and the walk of a man who has spent his life with horses. His daughter was thin and tired-looking, her face blotched with crying, but she had put on her best coat and hat and was clutching an enormous battered handbag.

'I've brought Mum's bag along,' she whispered. 'She can't bear to be parted from it, but they took her off in such a hurry.' They stood by the bed and looked speechlessly at the old lady, her nose high and pinched in her waxy face, the collar of the white gown much too big for her.

Chris wanted to look at her dressing, and the husband and daughter went obediently to wait in Sister's sitting-room.

Chris had her hand on Mrs Colley's wrist, frowning.

'Not long,' she said. 'I have to stand by and let someone just slip off like this. Here – stay with her a minute. That Appendix'll be out of bed if I don't give her morphia.'

The green-shaded light over the bed fell on the old woman's face. You could trace the outline of every bone in her skull and her nose was typically sharp and prominent, as if the face had fallen away from it. Her skin was cold and faintly damp, and her pulse no more than a tremor and then not even that. I listened for her breathing and called Chris over. 'She's dead.'

'I wouldn't swear to it,' she said, and stood pensively tapping her foot. 'Look, get the hypo. syringe and the coramine. It couldn't hurt to give her a shot.'

'I suppose I'd better call her people in,' she said despondently, when she had given the injection. 'Oh, damn, here's Chubby. What the hell does he want?' Chubby was Mr Soames, the little new House Surgeon, just out of the egg, with fluffy hair that never would lie down on his round head. He was on for all surgical cases tonight, and was just going round to see if it was all right for him to go to bed. As we watched Mrs Colley, one of her eyelids fluttered and for a moment her breathing was audible.

'My God,' said Chris suddenly. 'I wonder...' She clutched hold of Chubby's arm. 'Listen,' she whispered urgently, 'couldn't we give her an intravenous? Couldn't we try it? Sister said it wasn't any use, but I don't know. *Please*, Mr Soames, do let's try. It seems awful just not to do anything when she's still alive.'

'All right,' he said and laughed nervously. 'I'll have a shot if you like.'

'I'll go and lay up the trolley,' she gabbled. 'Don't go away – I'll have it ready by the time you've scrubbed up. You put the electric heat cradle over her,' she told me, 'and tell her people they can't come in for a sec.'

'Is she...?' asked the daughter, getting up as I went into the sitting-room. 'We're going to try something,' I said. 'It might not be any good, but...' The old man was watching me like a trusting dog.

I went to hold Mrs Colley's arm for Chris, while she bandaged it to the splint to keep it still. Mr Soames was regulating the drip of the saline, his face flushed with excitement, for it was the first intravenous he had done since he had been here. Sister Gilbert came along to see why we had not rung her yet to say that Mrs Colley had died.

'I'll do the round while I'm here,' she said. 'All right, don't bother to come with me, Nurse,' and she tiptoed off down the ward alone.

When she came back, she found the three of us wild with excitement. Mrs Colley's skin was still cold, but it was no longer clammy. You could hear her breathing now; you could distinctly feel her pulse.

'Of course, it might be only a momentary rally,' Sister said doubtfully, but she obviously didn't think that.

'Keep her warm,' said Chubby, putting on his white coat, his chick's hair on end. 'I'll come back when I've finished my round. Let me know at once if anything happens, and for God's sake keep that drip running.'

'Tidy her up,' said Sister, 'and let her people come in.' While I was rearranging the sheets to hide a little blood that Chubby had spilt in his haste, I kept touching Mrs Colley, to feel her skin gradually losing its marble chill. Suddenly she opened her eyes and looked at me accusingly. 'Me arm,' she whispered, 'what you done to me arm?'

'Now you've got to keep that arm still, d'you hear? Don't you dare move it.' She raised a grizzled eyebrow at me.

'Hoity-toity,' she said faintly.

The husband and daughter came in, breathless with hope, glancing uneasily at the bandaged arm rigidly outflung and the gibbet-like saline apparatus. 'She may not know you,' whispered Chris, and Mrs Colley unhooded one eye. 'Think I don't know Dad?' she mumbled. ''Ere, where's me 'andbag?'

Prayer

We ask for your blessing upon
the sick and those who take
care of them.

Auf Wiedersehen

Music

'Sheep May Safely Graze' by J S Bach arranged by John Williams
(from Bridges: Lotus Records WH 6015)

Reading

from Friedrich by Hans Peter Richter

Germany 1934

The school bell rang. At the last tone, Teacher Neudorf closed the book and stood up. Slowly, in thought, he walked towards us. He cleared his throat and said, 'The lesson is over – but please stay a little longer; I want to tell you a story. Anyone who wants to can go home though.'

We looked at each other quizically.

Herr Neudorf stepped to the window, turning his back to us. From his jacket pocket he drew a pipe and began to fill it, looking at the trees in the playground all the while.

Noisily we collected our things. We prepared our briefcases and satchels. But no one left the classroom. We all waited.

Awkwardly Herr Neudorf lit his pipe. With obvious enjoyment he blew a few puffs against the windows. Only then did he turn to face us. He surveyed the rows of seats. When he saw that all were still filled, he nodded to us with a smile.

All eyes focused on Herr Neudorf. We didn't talk. From the hall came the sounds of other classes. In one of the back benches someone shuffled his feet.

Herr Neudorf walked to the front row. He sat on one of the desks. His pipe glowing, he looked at each of us in turn and blew the smoke over our heads to the window.

We stared at our teacher, tense and expectant.

At last he began to speak in a calm, soft voice. 'Lately, you've heard a lot about Jews, haven't you?' We nodded. 'Well, today I also have reason to talk to you about Jews.'

We leaned forward to hear better. A few propped their chins on their schoolbags. There wasn't a sound.

Herr Neudorf directed a blue cloud of sweet-smelling smoke up to the ceiling. After a pause, he continued, 'Two thousand years ago all Jews lived in the land which is now called Palestine; the Jews call it Israel.

The Romans governed the country through their governors and

prefects. But the Jews did not want to submit to foreign rule and they rebelled against the Romans. The Romans smashed the uprising and in the year 70 after the birth of Christ destroyed the Second Temple in Jerusalem. The leaders of the revolt were banished to Spain or the Rhineland. A generation later, the Jews dared to rise again. This time the Romans razed Jerusalem to the ground. The Jews fled or were banished. They scattered over the whole earth. Years passed. Many gained wealth and understanding. Then came the Crusades.

Heathens had conquered the Holy Land and kept Christians from the holy places. Eloquent priests demanded the liberation of the Holy Grave; inflamed by their words, thousands of people assembled. But some declared 'What is the use of marching against the infidels in the Holy Land while there are infidels living in our midst?'

Thus began the persecution of the Jews. In many places they were herded together; they were murdered and burned. They were dragged by force to be baptized; those who refused were tortured.

Hundreds of Jews took their own lives to escape massacre. Those who could escape did so.

When the Crusades were over, impoverished sovereigns who had taken part in them had their Jewish subjects imprisoned and executed without trials and claimed their possessions.

Again, many Jews fled, this time to the East. They found refuge in Poland and Russia. But in the last century, there, too, they began to be persecuted.

The Jews were forced to live in ghettos, in isolated sections of towns. They were not allowed to take up so called 'honest' professions: they could not become craftsmen nor were they allowed to own houses or land. They were only allowed to work in trade and at money lending.'

The teacher paused, his pipe had gone out. He placed it in the groove for pens and pencils. He got off the desk and wandered about the classroom. He polished his glasses and continued:

'The Old Testament of the Christians is also the Holy Scripture of the Jews; they call it the Torah, which means "instruction". In the Torah is written down what God commanded Moses. The Jews have thought a great deal about the Torah and its commandments. How the laws of the Torah are to be interpreted they have put down in another very great work – the Talmud, which means "study".

Orthodox Jews still live by the law of the Torah. And that is not easy. The Torah, for instance, forbids the Jew to light a fire on the Sabbath or to eat the meat of unclean animals such as pigs.

The Torah prophesies the Jews' fate. If they break the holy laws, they will be persecuted and must flee, until the Messiah leads them back to their Promised Land, there to create His Kingdom among them. Because Jews did not believe Jesus to be the true Messiah, because they regarded him as an imposter like many before him, they crucified him. And to this day many people have not forgiven them for this. They believe the most absurd things about Jews; some only wait for the day when they can persecute them again.

There are many people who do not like Jews. Jews strike them as strange and sinister; they believe them capable of everything bad just because they don't know them well enough!'

Attentively we followed the account. It was so quiet that we could hear the soles of Herr Neudorf's shoes creak. Everyone looked at him; only Friedrich looked down at his hands.

'Jews are accused of being crafty and sly. How could they be anything else? Someone who must always live in fear of being tormented and hunted must be very strong in his soul to remain an upright human being.

It is claimed that the Jews are avaricious and deceitful. Must they not be both? Again and again, they have been robbed and dispossessed; again and again, they had to leave everything they owned behind. They have discovered that in case of need money is the only way to secure life and safety.

But one thing even the worst Jew-haters have to concede – the Jews are a very capable people! Only able people can survive two thousand years of persecution.

By always accomplishing more and doing it better than the people they lived among, the Jews gained esteem and importance again and again. Many great scholars and artists were and are Jews.

If today, or tomorrow, you should see Jews being mistreated, reflect on one thing – Jews are human beings, human beings like us!'

Without glancing at us, Herr Neudorf took up his pipe. He scraped the ashes out of the bowl and lit the remaining tobacco. After a few puffs, he said, 'Now I am sure you will want to know why I have told you all this, eh?'

He walked to Friedrich's seat and put a hand on his shoulder.

'One of us will leave our school today. It appears that Friedrich Schneider may no longer come to our school; he must change to a Jewish school because he is of the Jewish faith.

That Friedrich has to attend a Jewish school is no punishment, but only a change. I hope you will understand that and remain Friedrich's friends, just as I will remain his friend even though he will no longer be in my class. Friedrich may need good friends.'

Herr Neudorf turned Friedrich around by his shoulder. 'I wish you all the best, Friedrich!' the teacher said, 'and *Auf Wiedersehen!*'

Friedrich bent his head. In a low voice he replied, '*Auf Wiedersehen!*'

With quick steps Herr Neudorf hurried to the front of the class. He jerked up his right arm, the hand straight out at eye level, and said, 'Heil Hitler!'

We jumped up and returned the greeting in the same way.

The events described in this story were part of the process in Nazi Germany which ended with the killing of six million Jews. The Jews were first separated from non-Jews. Their businesses were destroyed or confiscated. Later they were put into concentration camps where they were systematically killed. The whole process was accompanied by a carefully worked out propaganda campaign in which the German people were indoctrinated to believe that the Jews were inferior to other people and that they were responsible for Germany's problems. All this was done under the leadership of Adolf Hitler.

Prayer

Let us bow our heads, close our eyes and think
quietly about the words we have just heard.
Have things changed very much?

I Remember

Music

'The Flame Trees of Thika' (from Reflections by Various Artists: CBS 40-10034)

Reading

'The Sound in the Night' by Sharmila Modha

I wonder what is your earliest memory and why you remember that incident, place or person? Some people have vivid memories about a life very different from the one they are leading now. This piece is written by a fourteen-year-old girl who recalls an incident from her early life when she lived a long way from these shores.

I was born in Kenya and I was a noisy lively baby. We lived near a game reserve in Nakuru, and I grew up with cubs and calves. Being a member of a large family I was very spoilt and pampered. I used to wake up in the middle of the night and demand to be picked up. My father would then take me outside, and sometimes even give me rides on our baby elephant, Jumbo.

As I grew up I became less pampered, and I grew to love all animals, even the baby crocodiles! It was lovely to sit out on the verandah and watch the setting sun, to hear the crickets noisily chirping away, the horses neighing and the elephants trumpeting. There was no way in which you could shut your mind to all the different sounds in the night. Even when you fell asleep you would dream to the moths whirring around the lamps, and the insects buzzing. I sometimes wonder at how much the people living in towns and cities miss. For one thing they never hear the birds singing, and they never seem to notice the brilliant sunsets. I feel sorry for them.

At the age of six, we moved away from Nakuru and went to live in a small village, near a vast sugar-cane plantation. Muhoroni was wonderful; all I missed was the animals. The night sounds were still there and the insects with lights, which the local people ate – raw! Even at night, after roosting time, you could still hear the chickens. The sound which I loved to hear most at night was my dad's snoring. If I could not get to sleep, all I had to do was to listen to my dad snoring and I'd soon fall asleep.

One night as I lay in bed listening to the sugar-canes swishing in the night breeze, I heard a sound which I'd never heard before. As I got up to investigate I saw shapes, human shapes, moving outside.

I tip-toed and woke my dad, who then woke my brothers in the next room, but by the time they were awake the robbers had already broken down the wooden door and turned on the lights. I was ushered under the bed with my sister, and the door was shut on us.

I will never forget that terrible night. The thieves took everything; the mattresses, the radio (we had no television) and even the tables and chairs. My brothers fought bravely, but they were nothing compared to men with shining axes. During the fight, my eldest brother had his head split open, and then the police came. This sent the thieves away and we never saw our belongings again. As for my brother, he was rushed to hospital, where he was unconscious for two days, after which he made a speedy recovery. What I still cannot believe is why our neighbours didn't hear the shouting and scream-ing, and come to our rescue. It was the worst night of my life, and I can still recall vividly all the details leading up to it and afterwards.

After the robbery my dad did not have very much money, for the thieves had obviously demanded that for my eldest sister's life. Thank God I had loving aunts and uncles who helped us.

Even now, in England, I still get very frightened when I hear noises in the night. I still have nightmares about that particular night even though it was seven years ago.

In Kenya it was always very noisy at night compared to England. Here when I go to sleep, I can faintly hear the television downstairs, and the occasional car that passes by. I never hear crickets or even the birds in the morning.

Prayer

Memories are the treasures of our life,
born from our experiences both good and
bad. May we appreciate the value to
be found in both.

Author Index

Anonymous   22, 33, 78, 82
Avery, Valerie   12

Barnard, Marius   30
Black, Virginia   80
Bode, Richard   20
Bombeck, Erma   18, 55
Bottomley, Lynn   51
Brooke, Avery   56
Burke, Carl   11

Chaplin, Sid   46
Cheston, Molly   57

Dickens, Monica   83
Dranginis, Rita   67

Godden, Rumer   25

Hamill, Pete   60

Kirk, Harvey   74
King, Martin Luther   8, 9

Lee, Laurie   10, 35
Lewis, C. Day   49
Lloyd, R.H.   40

Lynes, C.L.   69

Modha, Sharmila   90
Morris, Brian   16

Naughton, Bill   62
Nevill, E. Mildred   53

Ostreicher, Paul   9

Palmer, Lilli   27

Rae, Daphne   5
Rees, Jenny   42
Richter, Hans Peter   86
Rudley, Stephen   69

Singer, Isaac   71

Thomas, Dylan   44
Topping, Frank   43, 50, 77

Wager, Vanessa   64
Wallis, Karen   65
Warren, Hilda   14
Waterhouse, Keith   37
Winter, Tony   23

Index of Titles of Readings

Albert's Christmas Ship   37
An Episode of Sparrows (extract)   25
And God Created Mothers   18

Because You Are Like That   40

Change Lobsters and Dance (extract)   27
Christmas Landscape   35
Cider With Rosie (extract)   10

Dreams of Old Age   65

English Country Customs   80

Friedrich (extract)   86
From a Mother to her Child   55

Georgie and Grandpa   51
Genesis   16
Getting Away   14
Gran   12

Hearts of Oak   60
Holiday Memory   44

I Have a Dream   8

Incredible Human Body   74
Isn't It Lovely   23

Love Until it Hurts   5

Mother Often Annoyed Me   42
My Son, the Carpenter   20

One Pair of Feet (extract)   83
One Saturday   64
One Solitary Life   22
Our Secret and Some Other Day   33

Plea by a Retarded Child   67

Some Other Day and Our Secret   33

The Art of Marriage   82
The Day of the Sardine (extract)   46
The Goalkeeper's Revenge (extract)   62
The Heart of a Child   30
The Sound in the Night   90
The Unexploded Bomb   49
Thou Shalt Not Bear False Witness   76

To Parents, from their Children   53
Unforgettable Christy Brown   69
Value of a Smile   78
When it's Brave to be Chicken   57
Zlateh the Goat and Other Stories   71

Music Index

Air on the G String   30, 64
'All Good Gifts Around Us'   20
'All Things Bright and Beautiful'   16
'Annie's Song'   25

'Battle Hymn of the Republic'   8
'By the Sleepy Lagoon'   44

'Cagney and Lacey'   62
Canon in D Major   67, 69
'Cavatina'   22
'Christmas Song'   37

'Dad's Army'   49
'Day is Done'   14
'Doctor Kildare' Theme   83

'Friends Medley'   10

Gymnopedie No 1   27

'He's Got the Whole World . . .'   40

In the Bleak Midwinter   35

'Match of the Day'   74

'Memories of Summer'   33

Overture from *Fiddler on the Roof*   71
'Oxygene'   5

'Sheep May Safely Graze'   86
'She's Leaving Home'   53, 55
'Snowflakes are Dancing'   23
'Song of the Seashore'   18
Star Wars Main Theme   57
'Streets of London'   65

'The Easy Winners'   78
'The Flame Trees of Thika'   90
'The Times They are A-Changing'   46
'The Windmills of Your Mind'   76
Theme from *Love Story*   42
'Tie a Yellow Ribbon'   60

'When I'm Sixty Four'   12
Widor Toccata in F   80, 82
'Winter' from The Four Seasons   51

Subjects of Readings

Beginning (and ending)   10, 16
Blessing the bride   80
Children   10, 14, 18, 22, 23, 25, 30, 33, 44, 51, 53, 57
Christmas   35, 37
Communication   14, 27, 49
Dad (leaving home)   64
Dares   57
Dreams of old age   33, 65
Easter   22
Examples   5, 8, 42
Finder's keepers   62
Fool's paradise   71
Friendship   25, 43, 86
Genesis   16
Gentleness   5, 18, 25, 69
Gossip   76
Helplessness   5
Holidays   27, 44
Home   46, 60
Honesty   53, 62
Human body   74
Loneliness   18, 25

Love of life   42
Loving people   5, 16, 42, 82
Loyalty   40, 55
Marriage   60, 64, 69, 80, 82
Mothers   18, 42, 46, 55, 64
Nursing   5, 30, 33, 69, 83
Old age   12, 23, 33, 51, 65
Parents   14, 18, 37, 53, 55
Quality of character   5, 8, 22, 27
Quarrels   14, 46, 49
Relationships   14, 18, 33, 42, 46, 53, 55, 60, 65
Retarded child   67
Saying sorry   14
Smile   78
Talents   20
Trouble   14, 25, 40, 46, 86, 90
Understanding   8, 12, 14, 18, 33, 36, 51, 55, 64
Unexpected, The   60
Winter   23, 35
Wisdom of youth   20

Suggested Themes

Adventure

Change Lobsters and Dance   27
Holiday Memory   44
English Country Customs   80

Alone

The Heart of a Child   30
Dreams of Old Age   65

Anger and Quarrels

Getting Away   14
The Day of the Sardine   46
The Unexploded Bomb   49
One Saturday   64

Boasting

Genesis   16
When it's Brave to be Chicken   57
The Goalkeeper's Revenge   62

Communication

Change Lobsters and Dance   27
The Unexploded Bomb   49
To Parents, from their Children   53

Courage and Honesty

When it's Brave to be Chicken   57
The Goalkeeper's Revenge   62

Decision and Thinking

Zlateh the Goat   71
The Art of Marriage   82

Determination and Purpose

From a Mother to her Child   55
Hearts of Oak   60
Unforgettable Christy Brown   69
One Pair of Feet   83

Faith and Hope

Change Lobsters and Dance   27
Because You are Like That   40
Hearts of Oak   60

Family Scenes

Cider with Rosie   10
Getting Away   14
An Episode of Sparrows   25

To Parents, from their Children   53
When it's Brave to be Chicken   57
The Goalkeeper's Revenge   62
One Saturday   64
And God Created Mothers   18
My Son, the Carpenter   20
From a Mother to her Child   55
Unforgettable Christy Brown   69
Mother Often Annoyed Me   42
Holiday Memory   44
The Day of the Sardine   46
Value of a Smile   78
One Pair of Feet   83

Forgiveness and Apology

An Episode of Sparrows   25
The Day of the Sardine   46

Gossip

The Unexploded Bomb   49
Thou Shalt Not Bear False Witness   76

Giving

One Solitary Life   22
The Heart of a Child   30
Albert's Christmas Ship   37

Handicaps

Change Lobsters and Dance   27
Plea by a Retarded Child   67
Unforgettable Christy Brown   69

Kindness

Because You Are Like That   40
Georgie and Grandpa   51
The Art of Marriage   82

Love and Gentleness

And God Created Mothers   18
An Episode of Sparrows   25
Mother Often Annoyed Me   42
From a Mother to her Child   55
Hearts of Oak   60
Unforgettable Christy Brown   69

Memories

Some Other Day   33
Mother Often Annoyed Me   42
One Saturday   64
Dreams of Old Age   65

Need

The Heart of a Child   30
One Pair of Feet   83

Old Age

Gran   12
Change Lobsters and Dance   27
Some Other Day   33
Georgie and Grandpa   51
Dreams of Old Age   65

Paradise

Change Lobsters and Dance   27
Zlateh the Goat   71

Promise

Hearts of Oak   60
English Country Customs   80

Reward

Albert's Christmas Ship   37
Unforgettable Christy Brown   69
Value of a Smile   78

Seasons

One Solitary Life   22

Isn't it Lovely?   23
Christmas Landscape   35
Albert's Christmas Ship   37

Superman, Superwoman

Incredible Human Body   74

Talents

My Son, the Carpenter   20

Understanding

Some Other Day   33
The Day of the Sardine   46
To Parents, from their Children   53
Plea by a Retarded Child   67

Wisdom and Responsibility

Because You Are Like That   40
To Parents, from their Children   53
From a Mother to her Child   55
Zlateh the Goat   71
The Art of Marriage   82

Work and Play

Holiday Memory   44